Summer Desserts

ROSEMARY STARK,
EMMA CODRINGTON
AND
MICHAEL RAFFAEL

This edition first published 1988 by Hamlyn Publishing Group
Michelin House 81 Fulham Road London SW3 6RB
© 1986 Hennerwood Publications Limited
ISBN 0 600 55879 7
Printed in Hong Kong

Summer Desserts

Contents

Introduction

At its simplest a summer dessert is a dish of the fruit which is at its brightest, plumpest, sweetest and best in the garden or market, sugared if necessary and perhaps accompanied by a jug or bowl of cream. While such a simple dessert is just right for some summer days, there are other times when a more elaborate dish is required for entertaining or to crown a celebratory meal – a cake or meringue assembly perhaps, an airy mousse or a soufflé, hot, cold or iced; a homemade ice cream or sorbet or a colourful combination of fruits, possibly macerated in a spirited syrup.

Ice creams can prolong the season of summer fruits, capturing for some months the flavour of fruit when it is at its cheapest and best. But fruit ice creams are far more than just a convenient way of using up summer fruits, the addition of cream softens and enriches the fruit and these ices can be further enhanced and intensified with essences, distillations of flowers, cordials and liqueurs. There are fascinating combinations of flavour to be made with different fruits, and contrasts of texture can be provided by nuts and other crunchy additions. For a dinner party ice creams are a boon, since by their very nature they must be made in advance. Some ices can be kept in the freezer for as long as six months without deteriorating in quality.

It helps when making ice creams to know a little about the freezing process. A fruit purée on its own will freeze to a solid consistency like an iced lolly, but when other ingredients like sugar, fats, gelatine, eggs, alcohol and air are added to the purée they prevent it from freezing quite so hard. There are many good quality manufactured ice creams in the shops, but the surest way to an ice cream you can serve with pride is to make it yourself.

GRANITAS

Somewhere between an ice cream and a drink, granitas are usually served in tall glasses and eaten with a spoon. Sugar, and sometimes, alcohol, is used to impede the freezing process and the finished granita has a grainy texture as the ice granules are deliberately preserved. Granitas are sometimes layered with cream or laced with alcohol at the serving stage.

SORBETS

Like granitas, sorbets are made with a sugar syrup base to prevent them from freezing very hard, but they also contain beaten egg whites to aerate and lighten the mixture and to give a more finely grained texture.

CREAMY ICES

Cream ices contain fats, generally in the form of cream and egg custard. The classic ice cream is based on a rich egg custard. Usually these ices have a greater proportion of yolks to whites because yolks have a

higher fat content but sometimes, for example in the case of ice creams with a great deal of fruit, egg yolks only are used. Although whipped cream may be blended in, the custard formula does not include sufficient air to prevent ice granules forming, so these ices must be beaten during freezing to disperse any graininess which would spoil the rich, smooth texture of the finished dish.

SERVING ICES

Most ice creams require a period of softening after they are taken out of the freezer and this is usually done in the refrigerator so that the ice cream softens evenly all the way through. If an ice cream is to be served scooped out into balls, it can be more convenient to do the preliminary softening some hours beforehand. Chill the serving dish or dishes in the refrigerator while the ice cream softens, then scoop out the ice creams and arrange them neatly, then return the dish to the freezer. The serving dish must, of course, be freezer-proof and, if the ice cream is to be in the freezer for more than a couple of hours it should be lightly covered with film or the whole dish slipped into a freezer bag. Small scoops of ice cream do not take very long to soften to the optimum consistency, so they can be softened in a cool room, but remember to take the dish from the freezer ten minutes or so before you are going to serve it. It is at this stage that ices should be decorated.

FREEZER CONTAINERS

Pack ice creams into unbreakable freezer proof containers with covers to prevent evaporation and consequent freezer-burn. Desserts like iced soufflés, which are made in their serving dishes, can either be put into another, larger, covered container or covered with freezer film. Because they contain a lot of air, iced

soufflés melt quickly at room temperature, or even in the refrigerator, so they are best served straight from the freezer. Since it is important to the quality of an ice cream that it be frozen as quickly as possible, thinner containers, which conduct the cold faster, are preferable. Always freeze ice creams in the coldest part of the freezer, the fast-freeze chamber if your freezer has one. As many as possible of the container's surfaces should touch the floor and sides of the freezer, so rectangular containers are the best choice. Ice creams frozen in a bowl for ease of beating can be transferred to a covered box as soon as all the beatings are completed.

SUGAR

With every type of ice it is important to use the exact quantity of sugar specified in the recipe. This is because of the effect sugar has on the freezing process. Sometimes an unfrozen mixture may seem too sweet, but freezing always bleaches out sweetness and softens flavours. It is because of this 'bleaching' of taste that intensified flavours are so useful in ice cream making: concentrated fruit juices, cordials intended for dilution, citrus juices and distillations in the form of flower waters and liqueurs all sharpen flavour and counteract sweetness.

Sometimes a sugar syrup has to be incorporated into a mixture the moment it reaches a given stage, for example when ice creams are made by beating a sugar syrup into egg yolks: the heat partially cooks the yolks, and hard beating simultaneously incorporates air and swells the volume to a bulky mousse. However, the mixture must be cooled and preferably chilled before freezing. Since it is bad culinary practice to put warm mixtures into the refrigerator, raising the air temperature to the detriment of the other foods, plunging bowls and pans into iced water to cool them rapidly can be a

useful technique. When a custard has been made in a double boiler, you can simply tip out the boiling water from the base section, replace it with iced water and return the custard to the top section. A change of iced water halfway through the cooling process or, even two or three times, speeds it up.

For boiling sugar it is important to use a heavy-based pan that distributes heat evenly. All the sugar must dissolve before boiling point is reached, so you should stir it continually over low heat, washing down granules from the side of the pan with a brush dipped in cold water. When boiling point is reached no further stirring is necessary and you can raise the heat a little. Never leave a boiling syrup unattended: it may progress slowly towards the desired stage, then make a sudden rapid climb to achieve it. Vigilance is essential. When you are testing by the iced water method always take the pan right off the heat in case the correct stage has already been reached.

MERINGUES AND HOT SOUFFLÉS

A crisp, light meringue makes such a perfect sweet contrast to the sharpness of fruit and the smooth richness of cream that it is not surprising that meringues feature large in summer desserts. Meringue mixtures are often a component part of ice creams too, and they are of three basic types. The classic Swiss meringue is made by gradually whisking half the caster sugar into the beaten egg whites, then folding in the remainder all at once. For a more marshmallow-like meringue mixture that holds its shape reliably but remains sticky inside after cooking, all the caster sugar is beaten in very gradually, often a mere teaspoon at a time: this is the method used for French meringues and is ideal for pavlova cases. For Italian meringues, the most supple and robust of all the meringue mixtures, the sugar is boiled to hard ball stage and then poured immediately on to stiffly beaten egg whites, while whisking continually. Unlike French or Swiss meringue, this billowy Italian meringue will hold its shape and texture for some hours, but its surface remains sticky and its texture pliable during cooking. It is often used in ice cream making and for decorative dessert toppings, and is used to swathe ice creams to be made into alaskas.

Meringues containing nuts have a different texture from plain meringues, since the nuts release some oil in cooking. For this reason they make flatter shapes, perfect for crisp layers in assemblies of fruit and cream. An unbaked meringue mixture is often the basis of an iced or chilled soufflé, and for this the resilience of Italian meringue can be advantageous. A hot soufflé can make a lovely ending to a cold summer meal, but the timing of a soufflé that is to be served at the end of a meal is trickier than for one at the beginning. The basic mixture can, however, be made in advance, and the beaten egg white incorporated immediately before the soufflé goes into the preheated oven. It is always better to have guests wait expectantly for a soufflé than to expect the soufflé to fit a demanding dinner schedule.

Sugar Boiling

Sugar syrups are important in summer desserts and the most accurate way to identify the different stages when boiling sugar is to use a sugar thermometer. Below are the temperatures for the different stages and quick, alternative tests which can be used when a sugar thermometer is not available.

SMOOTH: 102-104°C/214-218°F
Dip a spoon into the syrup and allow it to cool for a moment or two. Rub a little syrup between the thumb and forefinger. The fingers should slide smoothly but the syrup should cling to the skin.

THREAD: 107°C/225°F
Using a small spoon remove a little of the syrup and allow it to fall from the spoon on to a dish. The syrup should form a fine thin thread.

SOFT BALL: 113-118°C/235-245°F
Drop a small amount of the syrup into iced water. Mould the sticky syrup into a soft ball with the fingers. Remove the ball from the water. It should immediately lose its shape.

FIRM BALL: 118-121°C/244-250°F
Drop a little syrup into iced water, then using the fingers mould into a ball. Remove the ball from the water. It should feel firm but pliable and fairly sticky.

HARD BALL: 120-130°C/248-266°F
Drop a little syrup into iced water, then using the fingers mould into a ball. Remove the ball from the water. It should feel resistant to the fingers and still feel quite sticky.

SOFT CRACK: 132-142°C/270-286°F
Drop a little syrup into iced water. Remove from the water and gently stretch it between the fingers. It should form hard but elastic strands, and only feel slightly sticky.

HARD CRACK: 149-154°C/300-310°F
Drop a little syrup into iced water. Remove from the water. It should form brittle threads which snap easily between the fingers, and no longer feel sticky.

CARAMEL: 160-177°C/320-350°F
Using a small spoon remove a little of the syrup and pour it on to a white saucer. The syrup should be a light golden brown colour.

Tutti Frutti

St. Clement's Special

ORANGE AND LEMON GRANITA

> Serves 4-6
> 50 g (2 oz) granulated sugar
> 300 ml (½ pint) water
> 300 ml (½ pint) orange juice
> 2 tablespoons lemon juice
> slices of orange, to decorate

Preparation time: *5 minutes, plus cooling and freezing*
Cooking time: *10 minutes*

1. Put the sugar and water in a heavy-based saucepan and stir over a low heat until the sugar dissolves. Raise the heat and boil fast, without stirring, for 5 minutes. Remove the pan from the heat and stir in the orange and lemon juices. Allow the mixture to cool, then chill in the refrigerator.
2. Pour the mixture into a shallow freezer tray and freeze for about 1-1½ hours until it is quite firm. Turn the frozen mixture into a roasting tin and, using a metal fork, break it up into tiny pieces. Spoon the crystals into a freezer bag, seal, and return to the freezer. F
3. Before serving, chill the glasses. 10 minutes before it is required take the bag of crystals from the freezer and spoon them into the chilled glasses. Decorate each one with a slice of orange fixed over the side. Chill in the refrigerator until serving.
F Freeze for 3 months.

Mango Tango

MANGO AND LIME SHERBET

> 1 large ripe mango
> 2 tablespoons fresh lime juice
> 150 ml (¼ pint) soured cream
> 2 egg whites
> 50 g (2 oz) caster sugar
> slices of lime, to decorate

Preparation time: *10 minutes, plus freezing*

1. Holding it over the goblet of a liquidizer or processor to catch all the juice, cut the mango into quarters and cut away all the flesh from the stone. Scrape the flesh from the skin of the mango into the goblet.
2. Place the lime juice and the cream in the liquidizer goblet and blend to a purée. Transfer the mixture to a freezer container.
3. Put the egg whites in a bowl and whip them until they hold soft peaks. Add the sugar, 1 teaspoon at a time, beating hard all the time. Fold the egg mixture into the mango mixture and freeze until firm without further beating. F
4. Serve in chilled glasses and decorate each one with slices of lime.
F Freeze for 3 months.

Morning Glory

GRAPEFRUIT SORBET

> Serves 4-6
> 75 g (3 oz) granulated sugar
> 300 ml (½ pint) water
> finely grated rind of 1 grapefruit
> 300 ml (½ pint) grapefruit juice
> 2 egg whites

Preparation time: *10 minutes, plus cooling and freezing*
Cooking time: *5 minutes*

1. Place the sugar and the water in a small heavy-based saucepan and stir over a low heat until the sugar dissolves. Bring to the boil and let the mixture bubble until it has reduced by half. Leave on one side to cool.
2. Stir the grapefruit rind and juice into the syrup. Transfer the mixture to a freezer container and freeze until mushy. This will take about 1-1½ hours.
3. Beat the egg whites until they are stiff. Beat the grapefruit mixture to break up the crystals, fold in the egg whites and freeze until firm. F Serve in chilled glasses.
F Freeze for 3 months.

FROM THE LEFT: Orange and lemon granita;
Mango and lime sherbet; Grapefruit sorbet.

Sweet William

HONEYED PEAR SORBET

450 g (1 lb) ripe dessert pears, peeled, cored and sliced
2 tablespoons lemon juice
2 tablespoons clear honey
2 egg whites
lemon julienne, to decorate

Preparation time: 15 minutes, plus cooling and freezing
Cooking time: 10 minutes

1. Place the pears in a medium saucepan with the lemon juice and honey. Cover and simmer gently until the fruit is soft.
2. Purée the pears in a blender. Allow the purée to cool, then spoon it into a freezer container and freeze for about 1½ hours until mushy.
3. Beat the egg whites until stiff. Beat the pear mixture to break up the ice crystals, then fold in the egg white and freeze until firm. F Decorate with lemon julienne.
F Freeze for 3 months.

Sailor's Saviour

GIN AND LIME SORBET

Serves 4-6
75 g (3 oz) granulated sugar
600 ml (1 pint) water
1 lime, thinly peeled
3 tablespoons fresh lime juice
3 tablespoons gin
2 egg whites
slices of fresh lime, to decorate

Preparation time: 10 minutes, plus cooling and freezing.
Cooking time: 15 minutes

1. Put the sugar, water and lime peel in a small heavy-based pan and stir over a low heat until the sugar dissolves. Bring the mixture to the boil and let it bubble up for 10-15 minutes until it has reduced by half. Leave on one side to cool.
2. Squeeze the juice from the lime and add it to the mixture together with the gin. Chill in the refrigerator, then strain into a freezer container and freeze for about 1 hour until partially frozen.
3. Beat the egg whites until stiff, then fold them into the chilled mixture and freeze until set. F
4. Serve in individual glasses and decorate with slices of fresh lime.
F Freeze for 3 months.

Market Garden

RHUBARB AND ORANGE ICE CREAM

Serves 4-6
450 g (1 lb) rhubarb, cut into 2.5 cm (1 inch) cubes
juice and finely grated rind of 2 oranges
75 g (3 oz) caster sugar
175 g (6 oz) can evaporated milk, chilled

Preparation time: 20 minutes, plus chilling and freezing
Cooking time: 15 minutes

Only use young tender sticks of rhubarb for this ice. When rhubarb gets older it becomes very acidic.

1. Place the rhubarb in a saucepan with the orange juice, cover, and cook gently until it is soft.
2. Stir in the sugar and cook for a further 2 minutes, uncovered. Purée the rhubarb in a blender until smooth. Leave to cool, then chill in the refrigerator.
3. Pour the evaporated milk into a bowl and whip to soft peaks. Beat in the orange rind. Fold in the rhubarb purée. Transfer the mixture to a freezer container and freeze until firm without further beating. F
F Freeze for 1 month.

FROM THE LEFT: Honeyed pear sorbet; Gin and lime sorbet.

Raspberry Blush

RASPBERRY FROMAGE BLANC

Serves 6
100 g (4 oz) low fat quark or fromage blanc
75 g (3 oz) caster sugar
300 ml (½ pint) double cream
225 g (8 oz) raspberries
a few fresh raspberries, to decorate

Preparation time: *15 minutes, plus freezing*

Quark is a slightly acidic creamed cottage cheese. It can be made with skimmed milk or may have a low fat base. Fromage blanc is a fresh cheese, also with a varying fat base, which can be used as a yoghurt substitute.

1. Put the quark into a bowl with the sugar and 2 tablespoons of the cream and beat together until smooth.
2. Using a fork, mash the raspberries to a chunky pulp and stir them into the quark.
3. Whip the remaining cream to soft peaks and fold it into the raspberry mixture. Transfer the mixture to a freezer container and freeze until firm, beating twice at hourly intervals to break up the ice crystals. F Serve decorated with fresh raspberries.
F Freeze for 3 months.

Forbidden Fruit

PASSION FRUIT ICE CREAM

Serves 6-8
3 passion fruit, halved
50 g (2 oz) granulated sugar
85 ml (3 fl oz) water
2 egg yolks, beaten
300 ml (½ pint) double cream

Preparation time: *20 minutes, plus cooling and freezing*
Cooking time: *10 minutes*

1. Scoop the flesh from the passion fruit and work it through a nylon sieve.
2. Put the sugar and the water in a small heavy-based pan and heat gently, stirring all the time, until the sugar dissolves. Bring to the boil, without stirring, and boil until it reaches thread stage, 107°C/225°F on a sugar thermometer (page 9).
3. Place the egg yolks in a bowl. Pour the hot syrup on to the egg yolks, a little at a time, beating continually. Continue beating hard until the mixture is thick and creamy. Leave on one side to cool.

4. Stir the passion fruit purée into the mixture. Whip the cream until it forms soft peaks and fold it in. Transfer the mixture to a freezer container and freeze until firm without further beating. F Serve decorated with herbs.
F Freeze for 6 months.

Fruit and Nut

CHERRY AND ALMOND ICE CREAM

Serves 6
150 ml (¼ pint) milk
50 g (2 oz) ground almonds
1 egg and 1 extra yolk
75 g (3 oz) caster sugar
2-3 drops almond essence
450 g (1 lb) red cherries, stoned
150 ml (¼ pint) double cream
25 g (1 oz) slivered almonds
a few fresh cherries, to decorate

Preparation time: *20 minutes, plus cooling and freezing*
Cooking time: *20 minutes*

1. Pour the milk into a small saucepan, stir in the ground almonds, bring to the boil then set aside.
2. Put the egg and the extra yolk in a heatproof bowl with the sugar and beat until pale and thick. Pour on the milk and almond mixture. Place the bowl over a pan of gently simmering water and stir until thick. Stir in the almond essence and leave to cool.
3. Liquidize the cherries in a blender, then stir them into the custard.
4. Toss the slivered almonds in a heavy dry pan over a low heat to toast them. Leave to cool.
5. Whip the cream until it forms soft peaks. Fold the cream into the cherry mixture. Transfer the mixture to a freezer container and freeze until firm, beating twice at hourly intervals. Stir the slivered almonds into the mixture at the last beating. A F Serve in individual glasses, decorated with fresh cherries.
A Toast the almonds the day before and store in an airtight jar.
F Freeze for 6 months.

FROM THE LEFT: Raspberry fromage blanc; Passion fruit ice cream; Cherry and almond ice cream.

Tutti Frutti

Spice Ice

CINNAMON PEAR ICE CREAM

450 g (1 lb) ripe pears, peeled, cored and chopped
2 tablespoons lemon juice
2 tablespoons golden syrup
50 g (2 oz) butter
1 teaspoon ground cinnamon
1 egg and 1 extra yolk
150 ml (¼ pint) double or whipping cream
pennyroyal mint leaves, to decorate

Preparation time: 20 minutes, plus cooling and freezing
Cooking time: 20 minutes

1. Place the pears in a saucepan with the lemon juice, golden syrup, butter and cinnamon. Bring slowly to the boil, then simmer uncovered until the pears are soft. Purée the pears in a blender and return the purée to the rinsed pan.
2. Put the egg and the extra yolk in a bowl and beat together. Stir the beaten eggs into the pear mixture, then place the pan over a very gentle heat and continue to stir until the mixture thickens. Leave on one side and allow the mixture to cool.
3. Transfer the pear mixture to a freezer container. Whip the cream until it forms soft peaks and fold it into the pear mixture. Freeze until firm, beating twice at hourly intervals. F Serve in individual dishes and decorate with mint leaves.
F Freeze for 6 months.

Harvester

BLACKBERRY AND APPLE ICE CREAM

Serves 8
900 g (2 lb) cooking apples, peeled, cored and roughly chopped
2 tablespoons lemon juice
225 g (8 oz) blackberries
150 g (5 oz) caster sugar
300 ml (10 fl oz) plain unsweetened yogurt, chilled
150 ml (¼ pint) double cream, chilled
To decorate:
a few blackberries
apple slices

Preparation time: 25 minutes, plus chilling and freezing
Cooking time: 15 minutes

1. Put the apples into a medium saucepan with the lemon juice and 2 tablespoons water, cover and cook over a gentle heat until the apples soften and begin to form a purée.
2. Stir in the blackberries and sugar and continue to cook for about 5 minutes until the juice runs out of the blackberries. Rub the mixture through a sieve and pour it into a freezer container. Chill for 1 hour in the refrigerator.
3. Stir the yogurt into the chilled mixture. Whip the cream until it forms soft peaks and fold it into the frozen mixture. Freeze until firm, beating twice at hourly intervals. Ⓕ
4. Serve in individual glass dishes and decorate with blackberries and apple slices.
Ⓕ Freeze for 6 months.

Devonshire Dairy

APPLE BUTTER ICE CREAM

Serves 6
750 g (1½ lb) cooking apples, peeled, cored and chopped
1 tablespoon lemon juice
50 g (2 oz) butter
75 g (3 oz) soft light brown sugar
300 ml (½ pint) plain unsweetened yogurt
150 ml (¼ pint) double cream

Preparation time: 20 minutes, plus chilling and freezing
Cooking time: 10 minutes

1. Place the apples in a saucepan with the lemon juice and 1 tablespoon water. Cover and cook for 5-10 minutes over a low heat, shaking the pan occasionally until the apples soften.

2. Cut the butter into small pieces and whisk into the apple purée. Whisk in the sugar. Leave to cool, then chill in the refrigerator for 1 hour.
3. Stir the yogurt into the apple purée. Transfer the mixture to a freezer container and freeze for 1 hour until stiff round the edges.
4. Whip the cream until it forms soft peaks. Using a fork, beat the partially frozen mixture to break up the crystals. Fold in the cream. Freeze until firm, beating twice at hourly intervals. Ⓕ
Ⓕ Freeze for 6 months.

Sharpshooter

MINTED BLACKCURRANT ICE CREAM

Serves 6-8
225 g (8 oz) blackcurrants, trimmed and washed
large sprig of mint
150 ml (¼ pint) milk
1 egg and 2 extra yolks
75 g (3 oz) caster sugar
300 ml (½ pint) double or whipping cream
mint flowers and leaves, to decorate

Preparation time: 20 minutes, plus cooling and freezing
Cooking time: 20 minutes

1. Put the blackcurrants into a saucepan with the mint buried in the middle. Pour on the milk, bring to the boil, cover and leave to cool.
2. Remove the mint and purée the fruit with the milk in a blender. Pass the purée through a nylon sieve to remove the pips. Return the purée to the rinsed pan and bring back to the boil.
3. Meanwhile place the egg, the extra yolks and the sugar in a heatproof bowl and whisk until pale and thick. Pour on the blackcurrant mixture. Put the bowl over a pan of gently simmering water and stir until it thickens, then remove from the heat and leave to cool.
4. Whip the cream until it forms soft peaks and fold it in. Transfer the blackcurrant mixture to a freezer container and freeze until firm, beating twice at hourly intervals. Ⓕ Serve in individual glass dishes and decorate with mint flowers and leaves.
Ⓕ Freeze for 6 months.

FROM THE LEFT: Cinnamon pear ice cream; Blackberry and apple ice cream; Minted blackcurrant ice cream.

Plum Crazy

PLUM GIN ICE CREAM

Serves 6-8
450 g (1 lb) red plums, halved and stoned
2 tablespoons gin
100 g (4 oz) granulated sugar
2 egg whites
150 ml (¼ pint) double or whipping cream

Preparation time: *20 minutes, plus freezing*
Cooking time: *25 minutes*

1. Put the plums in a saucepan with 1 tablespoon water, cover, and simmer until soft. Measure out 4 tablespoons juice and reserve. Place the fruit with the rest of the juice and the gin in a liquidizer and blend to a purée.
2. Place the sugar and the reserved juice in a heavy-based pan and boil to hard ball stage, 120°C/248°F on a sugar thermometer (page 9).
3. Meanwhile, put the egg whites in a medium bowl and beat them until they hold stiff peaks. Slowly pour the boiling syrup on to the beaten egg whites, beating hard all the time. Continue beating until the mixture cools. Fold the plum purée into the cooled mixture. Pour the cream into a medium bowl and whip until it forms soft peaks, then fold it into the mixture. Transfer the mixture to a freezer container and freeze until firm without further beating. F
F Freeze for 6 months.

Prune Smasher

PRUNE ARMAGNAC ICE CREAM

Serves 8-10
225 g (8 oz) packet pitted, ready-to-eat prunes
3 tablespoons Armagnac
225 g (8 oz) granulated sugar
150 ml (¼ pint) water
2 egg whites
300 ml (½ pint) double cream

Preparation time: *15 minutes, plus freezing*
Cooking time: *10 minutes*

Armagnac, the 'liquid gold of Gascony' is a smooth, velvety brandy of very high quality made in the south west of France and generally regarded as being second only to the very best Cognac. Armagnac is of much more ancient origin than Cognac. It combines very well with fruit in desserts and preserves.

1. Purée the prunes with the Armagnac in a blender or food processor.
2. Place the sugar and the water in a small saucepan and stir over a low heat until the sugar dissolves, then boil, without stirring, to hard ball stage, 120°C/248°F on a sugar thermometer (see page 9).
3. Meanwhile, beat the egg whites until stiff in a medium bowl, then pour on the hot syrup in a thin stream, beating hard all the time, continuing to beat until the mixture is cool. Transfer the mixture to a freezer container.
4. Whip the cream in a bowl until it forms soft peaks. There is no need to scrape off any meringue that clings to the beaters – it will whip into the cream. Stir the prune purée into the meringue mixture, then fold in the cream. Cover and freeze until firm without further beating. F
F Freeze for 6 months.

Double Red

RASPBERRY AND REDCURRANT ICE CREAM

Serves 6
100 g (4 oz) granulated sugar
3 tablespoons water
1 egg white
350 g (12 oz) raspberries
2 tablespoons redcurrant jelly
300 ml (½ pint) double or whipping cream

Preparation time: *15 minutes, plus freezing*
Cooking time: *10 minutes*

1. Put the sugar and water into a small heavy-based saucepan and stir over a gentle heat until the sugar dissolves. Bring to the boil, then boil without stirring until it reaches hard ball stage, 120°C/248°F on a sugar thermometer (page 9).
2. Place the egg white in a bowl and beat until stiff, then pour on the boiling syrup in a thin stream, beating hard until the mixture cools.
3. Purée the raspberries with the jelly in a blender. Strain the raspberry purée through a sieve and stir it into the meringue mixture.
4. Whip the cream until it forms soft peaks and fold it into the mixture. Transfer the mixture to a freezer container and freeze until firm without further stirring. F
F Freeze for 6 months.

FROM THE TOP: Plum gin ice cream; Prune armagnac ice cream; Raspberry and redcurrant ice cream.

Tutti Frutti

Tangerine Dreams

FROZEN TANGERINE CREAMS

Serves 6
8 large, loose-skinned tangerines or satsumas
1 tablespoon lemon juice
1 egg and 1 extra yolk
100 g (4 oz) caster sugar
300 ml (½ pint) double or whipping cream
evergreen leaves, to decorate

Preparation time: *35 minutes, plus cooling and freezing*
Cooking time: *15-20 minutes*

If you have any ice cream left over after filling the tangerine cups, store it in the freezer for another time.

1. Finely grate the rind from 2 of the tangerines. Cut off the tops from the remaining 6 tangerines and reserve. Using a curved grapefruit knife or a sharp-edged teaspoon, scoop out the tangerine flesh.
2. Put the flesh into a strainer and press out the juice. Measure the juice and if it is less than 300 ml (½ pint), make it up to this quantity by squeezing the juice from the 2 tangerines whose skins you have grated. Ⓐ Pour the juice into a small heavy-based saucepan. Add the lemon juice and bring the juices to the boil.
3. Meanwhile, put the egg, the extra yolk and the sugar into a heatproof bowl and beat until the mixture is thick and pale.
4. Pour the boiling juice on to the egg mixture in a thin stream, beating all the time. Place the bowl over a pan of boiling water and stir until the mixture thickens to a custard. Leave to cool, then chill in the refrigerator.
5. Whip the cream until it forms soft peaks, then fold it into the chilled custard. Transfer the mixture to a freezer container, cover and freeze, beating twice at hourly intervals. Ⓕ
6. Arrange the tangerine shells on a baking sheet and chill thoroughly in the refrigerator.
7. Two hours before serving, transfer the ice cream to the refrigerator to soften for 35-40 minutes. Using a metal spoon fill the shells with ice cream and replace the tops. Brush the skins with cold water to frost them and return them to the freezer.
8. 10 minutes before serving, transfer the tangerines to the refrigerator. Serve the tangerines on a large dish, strewn with glossy evergreen leaves.
Ⓐ Prepare the tangerine cups and the juice the day before and keep in the refrigerator.
Ⓕ Freeze for 6 months.

FROM THE TOP: Peach ice cream; Frozen tangerine creams.

Honey B

HONEYED BANANA ICE CREAM WITH NUTS

450 g (1 lb) bananas, peeled
2 tablespoons lemon juice
3 tablespoons thick honey
150 ml (¼ pint) plain unsweetened yogurt
50 g (2 oz) chopped nuts
150 ml (¼ pint) double cream
2 egg whites

Preparation time: *15 minutes, plus freezing*

1. Put the bananas in a bowl with the lemon juice and mash until smooth. Stir in the honey, then the yogurt and nuts and beat together well.
2. Whip the cream until it forms soft peaks and fold it into the banana mixture. Transfer the mixture to a freezer container and freeze until partially set.
3. Whisk the egg whites until stiff. Beat the banana mixture, then fold in the whites and freeze until firm. Ⓕ
Ⓕ Freeze for 3 months.

Sundown

PEACH ICE CREAM

Serves 6-8
4 large, ripe peaches (total weight about 750 g (1½ lb), skinned
50 g (2 oz) icing sugar
1 tablespoon lemon juice
2 tablespoons white wine
2 teaspoons gelatine
4 egg yolks
300 ml (½ pint) double cream

Preparation time: *20 minutes, plus cooling and freezing*
Cooking time: *15 minutes*

1. Quarter peaches and purée the flesh with the sugar.
2. Mix together the lemon juice and the wine in a small bowl and sprinkle on the gelatine.
3. Transfer the peach purée to a heatproof bowl. Beat in the egg yolks. Place the bowl over a pan of gently simmering water and stir until it thickens slightly.
4. Put the bowl of gelatine mixture into a shallow pan of hot water and stir until it dissolves. Stir the gelatine into the peach mixture and leave to cool.
5. Whip the cream until it forms soft peaks then fold it into the mixture. Transfer it to a freezer container. Freeze until firm, beating twice at hourly intervals. Ⓕ
Ⓕ Freeze for 6 months.

Tutti Frutti

Orange Blossom

FRESH ORANGE ICE CREAM

Serves 6
juice and finely grated rind of 2 medium oranges
1 egg, separated, and 1 extra yolk
50 g (2 oz) caster sugar
1 teaspoon gelatine
1 tablespoon water
150 ml (¼ pint) plain unsweetened yogurt, chilled
1 tablespoon orange flower water
150 ml (¼ pint) double or whipping cream, chilled
kumquats, sliced, to decorate

Preparation time: 20 minutes, plus chilling and freezing
Cooking time: 15 minutes

1. Put the orange juice and rind, the egg yolks and the sugar in a heatproof bowl over a pan of simmering water and stir with a wooden spoon until the mixture thickens. (It will not coat the back of the spoon in the same way as a creamy custard, but you will notice some thickening after 10 minutes or so.)
2. Meanwhile, sprinkle the gelatine on to the cold water in a small heatproof bowl. When you remove the bowl of orange custard, stand the bowl of gelatine in the pan of simmering water and stir until it dissolves, pausing to stir the custard now and again to prevent a skin forming on the surface.
3. Stir the gelatine into the custard with the yogurt and the orange flower water. Cool, then chill in the refrigerator for about 1 hour until the custard is on the point of setting.
4. Place the cream in a mixing bowl and whisk until it forms soft peaks, then whip the custard. Fold the cream into the custard, transfer the mixture to a freezer container and freeze for 1 hour until it is beginning to set round the edges.
5. Whip the egg white until it forms stiff peaks. Beat the custard. Fold the egg white into the custard, cover and freeze until firm. F Serve in chilled individual dishes and decorate with slices of kumquat or orange.
F Freeze for 6 months.

Cold Comfort

GOOSEBERRY ICE CREAM

Serves 6-8
450 g (1 lb) gooseberries, topped and tailed
200 g (7 oz) caster sugar
4 eggs, separated
300 ml (½ pint) double or whipping cream
few drops of green food colouring (optional)

Preparation time: 25 minutes plus cooling and freezing
Cooking time: 10 minutes

1. Put the gooseberries in a heavy-based pan with 3 tablespoons water and 75 g (3 oz) of the sugar. Stew very gently for about 10 minutes until the fruit is soft and pulpy. Purée in a liquidizer or blender and then sieve to remove the pips, or rub the fruit through a nylon sieve to produce a thick purée. Leave on one side to cool, then chill for 1 hour in the refrigerator.
2. In a large bowl whisk the egg whites until they are stiff, then whisk in the remaining sugar, a little at a time, until the whites are glossy.
3. Whip the cream until it forms soft peaks. Place the egg yolks in another bowl and beat well. Fold the cream into the meringue mixture and stir in the egg yolks and the cooled purée adding a few drops of green colouring, if necessary. Transfer the mixture to a freezer container and freeze until firm without further beating. F
F Freeze for 6 months.

Caribbean Cooler

LIME CORDIAL ICE CREAM

Serves 4-6
2 tablespoons granulated sugar
2 tablespoons lemon juice
3 tablespoons lime cordial
2 egg yolks
300 ml (½ pint) double or whipping cream
slices of lime, to decorate

Preparation time: 10 minutes, plus freezing
Cooking time: 15 minutes

1. Put the granulated sugar and the lemon juice in a heavy-based pan and stir over a gentle heat until the sugar dissolves, then bring to the boil without stirring and boil to soft ball stage, 113°C/235°F on a sugar thermometer (page 9).
2. Add the lime cordial, stir, and continue to boil until the mixture is syrupy.
3. Meanwhile, beat the egg yolks in a bowl, then pour on the hot syrup, a little at a time, beating continually until the mixture is cool, thick and creamy. Transfer the mixture to a freezer container.
4. Whip the cream and fold it in. Cover and freeze until firm without further stirring. F Serve in individual dishes and decorate with slices of lime.
F Freeze for 6 months.

FROM THE TOP: Fresh orange ice cream; Lime cordial ice cream.

Fairground Fancy

TOFFEE APPLE ICE CREAM

Serves 6
450 g (1 lb) cooking apples
25 g (1 oz) butter
50 g (2 oz) granulated sugar
250 ml (8 fl oz) water
2 egg yolks
300 ml (½ pint) double or whipping cream

Preparation time: *20 minutes, plus freezing*
Cooking time: *30 minutes*

1. Peel, core and roughly chop the apples. Put them in a heavy saucepan with 1 tablespoon water, cover, and heat gently until they form a purée. Cut the butter into small pieces and beat it into the purée. Continue beating until the purée is smooth. Leave to cool.
2. Put the sugar and 150 ml (¼ pint) of the water into a small heavy-based saucepan and stir continuously over a low heat until the sugar dissolves completely. Bring to the boil, then leave the mixture to bubble until it turns a deep, golden brown, then remove the pan from the heat immediately. Pour on the remaining water and stir until the caramel dissolves. Return the pan to the heat and boil until the sauce becomes syrupy and reduces by half.
3. Meanwhile, beat the egg yolks in a large bowl until they are thick and pale. Continue beating and pour on the hot caramel sauce in a thin stream and beat until the mixture cools.
4. Place the cream in a bowl and whip until it forms soft peaks. Fold the apple purée and the whipped cream into the egg mixture, then transfer the mixture to a freezer container. Cover and freeze until firm without further beating. F
F Freeze for 6 months.

Bananamost

BANANA ICE CREAM
WITH A HINT OF RASPBERRY

Serves 4-6
3 large, ripe bananas
1 tablespoon lemon juice
1 tablespoon raspberry jam, sieved
1 × 175 g (6 oz) can evaporated milk, chilled
25 g (1 oz) caster sugar
a few fresh raspberries, to decorate

Preparation time: *10 minutes, plus freezing*

1. Purée or mash the bananas until smooth and put them into a bowl. Add the lemon juice and raspberry jam and mix thoroughly.
2. Whip the evaporated milk until it forms soft peaks. Whip in the sugar and fold into the banana mixture. Transfer the mixture to a freezer container and freeze until firm without further beating. F Serve in individual dishes and decorate with fresh raspberries.
F Freeze for 1 month.

Garden Glory

GREENGAGE ICE CREAM

Serves 6-8
450 g (1 lb) greengages
1 tablespoon lemon juice
75 g (3 oz) soft light brown sugar
1 whole egg, separated, and 1 extra yolk
150 ml (¼ pint) double cream

Preparation time: *20 minutes, plus chilling and freezing*
Cooking time: *20 minutes*

1. Put the greengages in a pan with the lemon juice, cover and simmer gently until they are very soft. Sieve the greengages into a heatproof bowl.
2. Stir the sugar into the greengage pulp, then stir in the egg yolks. Place the bowl over a pan of gently simmering water and stir until the mixture thickens. Remove from the heat and leave on one side to cool then chill in the refrigerator for 1 hour. A
3. Whip the cream until it forms soft peaks and fold it into the greengage mixture. Transfer the mixture to a freezer container and freeze for about 1 hour until firm round the edges.
4. Beat the egg white until it is stiff. Beat the greengage mixture with a fork to combine the frozen and partially frozen areas. Fold in the egg white, return to the freezer and freeze until firm. F Serve in individual glasses accompanied by fan biscuits.
A Prepare the greengage mixture 24 hours ahead and refrigerate until needed.
F Freeze for 6 months.

FROM THE LEFT: Banana ice cream with a hint of raspberry; Greengage ice cream.

Fancy Flavours

Green Devil

CRÈME DE MENTHE SORBET

Serves 6
225 g (8 oz) granulated sugar
600 ml (1 pint) water
4 tablespoons lemon juice
1 miniature bottle mint liqueur
2 egg whites
green food colouring (optional)

Preparation time: *10 minutes, plus cooling and freezing*
Cooking time: *15 minutes*

1. Put the sugar and the water in a heavy-based pan and dissolve the sugar over a low heat, stirring all the time, then boil until reduced to 450 ml (¾ pint) syrup. Leave to cool.
2. Stir in the lemon juice and the mint liqueur, then transfer to a freezer container and freeze until partially frozen.
3. Place the egg whites in a bowl and beat until stiff. Take the partially frozen mixture from the freezer and beat until smooth. Fold in the egg whites with a metal spoon, adding a few drops of food colouring if you want to intensify the colour of the sorbet.
4. Freeze until firm. ⨍ Serve in chilled glasses.
⨍ Freeze for 3 months.

Country Cousin

BLACKCURRANT LEAF SORBET

Serves 4-6
225 g (8 oz) granulated sugar
600 ml (1 pint) water
20 young blackcurrant leaves
6 tablespoons lemon juice
2 egg whites
small sprigs of blossom, to decorate

Preparation time: *10 minutes, plus cooling and freezing*
Cooking time: *15 minutes*

1. Place the sugar and the water in a heavy-based pan and bring gently to the boil, stirring all the time until the sugar has dissolved. Put the blackcurrant leaves in the pan and simmer for 5 minutes, then leave to cool.
2. Stir the lemon juice into the syrup. Strain the mixture into a freezer container and freeze until mushy and partially frozen round the edges.
3. Place the egg whites in a bowl and beat until stiff. Transfer the frozen mixture to a bowl and beat until smooth, then fold in the egg whites. Return the mixture to the freezer container and freeze until firm. ⨍
4. Serve in chilled individual dishes, and decorate with blackcurrant blossoms.
⨍ Freeze for 3 months.

White Witch

WHITE WINE SORBET

Serves 4-6
225 g (8 oz) granulated sugar
600 ml (1 pint) water
2 tablespoons orange juice
2 tablespoons lemon juice
½ bottle Riesling
2 egg whites
small seedless black or white grapes, to decorate

Preparation time: *10 minutes, plus cooling and freezing*
Cooking time: *15 minutes*

1. Put the sugar and water in a heavy-based saucepan and stir over a low heat until the sugar dissolves, then boil until reduced to 300 ml (½ pint). Leave to cool.
2. Transfer the syrup to a freezer container and stir in the fruit juices and wine, then freeze until partially set.
3. Beat the egg whites until stiff. Remove the wine mixture from the freezer and beat until it is smooth. Fold in the egg whites and freeze until firm. ⨍
4. Serve the sorbet in chilled glasses and decorate with tiny bunches of grapes.
⨍ Freeze for 2 months.

FROM THE LEFT: Crème de menthe sorbet; White wine sorbet.

Pacific Sunset

ORANGE AND PASSION FRUIT GRANITA

Serves 4-6
1 × 175 ml (6 fl oz) carton frozen orange and passion fruit
  concentrate
4-6 teaspoons Grenadine

Preparation time: *5 minutes, plus freezing*

1. Pour the concentrated fruit juice into a freezer container and make it up with 2 cartons of cold water, rather than the 3 cartons recommended on the label. Freeze until almost hard.
2. Tip the frozen juice into a roasting tin and, using a metal fork, break it up into small pieces. Spoon the crystals into a freezer bag, fasten, and return to the freezer until required. ⅁
3. To serve, first chill 4 tall glasses in the refrigerator for about 15-20 minutes, then spoon some of the frozen crystals into each glass and top each portion with 1 teaspoon of Grenadine.
⅁ Freeze for 2 months.

Sicilian Whispers

COFFEE GRANITA WITH CREAM

Serves 8
75 g (3 oz) finely ground coffee
50 g (2 oz) demerara sugar
1 litre (1¾ pints) boiling water
300 ml (½ pint) whipping cream, chilled
2 teaspoons caster sugar

Preparation time: *10 minutes, plus cooling and freezing*

1. Mix the coffee and demerara sugar in a jug, pour on the boiling water and leave for 4 minutes, then stir thoroughly. Leave to infuse until cold.
2. Strain the coffee into a shallow freezer tray, chill, then freeze for about 1-1½ hours until just firm.
3. Turn the coffee block into a roasting tin and break up with a fork. Spoon the crystals into a heavy polythene bag, seal, and return to the freezer. ⅁
4. Before serving, chill the glasses. Transfer the coffee crystals from the freezer to the refrigerator 10 minutes before required.
5. Whip the cream in a bowl with the caster sugar. Spoon 2 alternate layers of coffee crystals and 2 of cream into each glass, beginning with coffee and finishing with cream.
⅁ Freeze for 2 months.

Braziliano

COFFEE ICE CREAM

Serves 4-6
300 ml (½ pint) milk
1 tablespoon demerara sugar
25 g (1 oz) finely ground coffee or 1 tablespoon instant coffee
  granules
1 egg and 2 extra yolks
300 ml (½ pint) double or whipping cream, chilled
1 tablespoon caster sugar

Preparation time: *15 minutes, plus chilling and freezing*
Cooking time: *20 minutes*

1. Place the milk and demerara sugar in a pan and heat to boiling point. Remove from the heat. Sprinkle on the ground coffee or add the coffee granules and leave on one side for 2 minutes. Stir, cover and allow to cool.
2. Put the egg and the extra yolks into a heatproof bowl and beat until thick and pale.
3. Strain the coffee-flavoured milk into the rinsed pan and reheat to boiling point, then pour it on to the eggs in a steady stream, beating hard all the time. Place the bowl over a pan of gently simmering water and stir until thickened. Leave to cool, then chill in the refrigerator.
4. Whip the cream with the caster sugar. Fold it into the coffee mixture and turn into a freezer container. Cover and freeze until firm, beating twice at hourly intervals. ⅁
⅁ Freeze for 6 months.

When you are making coffee to use as a flavouring, always make a very strong, concentrated brew and, whatever method you use, make sure that the coffee is strained or filtered really thoroughly. Coffee granita is an Italian speciality and the Italians make it using dark roasted coffee beans, sometimes known as continental blend. It is the custom in many Italian households to put sweetened left-over coffee in the freezer, ready for making granitas and iced coffee.

FROM THE LEFT: Orange and passion fruit granita; Coffee granita with cream.

Roman Holiday

APRICOT AMARETTO ICE CREAM

Serves 6-8
225 g (8 oz) dried apricots
2 tablespoons Amaretto di Saronno
150 ml (¼ pint) double or whipping cream
100 g (4 oz) granulated sugar
150 ml (¼ pint) water
2 egg whites

Preparation time: *20 minutes, plus soaking overnight, cooling and freezing*
Cooking time: *25 minutes*

Amaretto di Saronno is an Italian liqueur made from apricots and almonds.

1. Soak the apricots overnight in cold water to cover. Place the apricots and the soaking water in a pan, cover and simmer gently for 15 minutes or until soft.
2. Drain the apricots and liquidize to a purée. Allow to cool, then transfer to a medium bowl and stir in the liqueur. Whip the cream until it forms soft peaks, then fold it into the apricot purée.
3. Place the sugar and the water in a heavy-based pan and heat gently until the sugar dissolves, stirring all the time, then boil without stirring to hard ball stage, 120°C/248°F on a sugar thermometer (page 9).
4. Meanwhile, put the egg whites into a bowl and beat until stiff. Slowly pour on the boiling syrup, beating the egg whites at high speed all the time and continuing to beat until cool. Transfer the mixture to a freezer container. Fold in the apricot mixture and freeze until firm without further beating. F Serve with biscuits.
F Freeze for 3 months.

Blackcurrant Beauty

KIR ICE CREAM

Serves 4-6
1 whole egg and 2 extra yolks
75 g (3 oz) caster sugar
¼ bottle medium-sweet white wine
3 tablespoons Crème de Cassis
300 ml (½ pint) double cream
sprig of borage, to decorate

Preparation time: *15 minutes, plus chilling and freezing*
Cooking time: *5 minutes*

Kir, the refreshing combination of the blackcurrant liqueur, Crème de Cassis and chilled white wine, takes its name from Canon Kir, a Resistance hero and former Mayor of Dijon, the centre of a region of France where blackcurrants are a major crop.

1. Place the egg and the extra yolks in a bowl with the sugar and beat until pale and thick. Meanwhile, heat the white wine to boiling point.
2. Continue beating the egg and sugar mixture and pour on the wine. Add the Crème de Cassis, leave to cool, then chill in the refrigerator.
3. Transfer the cooled mixture to a freezer container. Beat the cream until thick and fold it in, then return the mixture to the freezer and freeze until firm, beating twice at hourly intervals. F Serve in individual glasses and decorate with fresh herbs.
F Freeze for 6 months.

Sherry-Cherie

FROZEN EGGNOG

Serves 2
2 egg yolks
75 g (3 oz) caster sugar
2 tablespoons cream sherry
300 ml (½ pint) double or whipping cream
sweet cicely, to decorate

Preparation time: *10 minutes, plus freezing*
Cooking time: *10 minutes*

For a romantic dinner, freeze this ice cream in heart-shaped moulds.

1. Place the egg yolks, sugar and sherry in a bowl over a pan of boiling water and beat until thick and creamy. Remove the bowl from the heat and continue beating until the mixture is cool. Transfer the mixture to a freezer container.
2. Whip the cream to soft peaks, then fold it into the mixture and freeze until firm without further beating. F Decorate each portion with fresh herbs.
F Freeze for 6 months.

CLOCKWISE FROM THE TOP: Apricot Amaretto ice cream; Kir ice cream; Frozen eggnog.

Scheherazade

PISTACHIO ICE CREAM

Serves 4-6
300 ml (½ pint) single cream
1 egg and 2 extra yolks
75 g (3 oz) caster sugar
50 g (2 oz) shelled pistachio nuts, coarsely chopped
150 ml (¼ pint) double or whipping cream, chilled

Preparation time: *15 minutes, plus chilling and freezing*
Cooking time: *15 minutes*

1. Pour the single cream into a saucepan and scald by heating it to just below boiling point.
2. Place the egg and the extra yolks in a heatproof bowl with the sugar and beat until thick and creamy. Pour on the hot cream. Place the bowl over a pan of gently simmering water and stir until thickened. Transfer the mixture to a freezer container and stir in the chopped nuts. Leave to cool, then chill in the refrigerator.
3. Whip the cream, then fold it into the chilled mixture. Cover and place in the freezer, removing to beat twice at hourly intervals. F
F Freeze for 6 months.

American Dream

PECAN AND MAPLE SYRUP ICE CREAM

Serves 6
2 eggs, separated
100 g (4 oz) granulated sugar
150 ml (¼ pint) water
2 tablespoons maple syrup
300 ml (½ pint) double or whipping cream
100 g (4 oz) shelled pecan nuts, roughly chopped

Preparation time: *15 minutes, plus freezing*
Cooking time: *10 minutes*

If you cannot get pecan nuts, make this ice cream with walnuts instead.

1. Put the egg whites into a large bowl and the yolks into a small one.
2. Place the sugar and the water in a heavy pan and stir over a low heat until the sugar melts, then, without stirring, boil to hard ball stage, 120°C/248°F on a sugar thermometer (page 9).
3. Meanwhile, beat the egg whites until they are stiff. Pour the boiling syrup on to them in a thin stream,
beating hard all the time, and continue beating until the mixture cools.
4. Mix the maple syrup into the egg yolks. In another bowl whip the cream to soft peaks and stir in the nuts and the maple syrup mixture. Fold into the meringue mixture, transfer to a freezer container, cover and freeze until firm without further beating. F Serve with wafer biscuits.
F Freeze for 6 months.

Cool Crunch

CARAMEL WALNUT ICE CREAM

Serves 6-8
50 g (2 oz) granulated sugar
10 tablespoons water
2 egg yolks, beaten
300 ml (½ pint) double or whipping cream
50 g (2 oz) shelled walnuts, coarsely chopped

Preparation time: *10 minutes, plus freezing*
Cooking time: *20 minutes*

1. Put the sugar and 5 tablespoons of water into a heavy-based saucepan and stir gently over a low heat until the sugar dissolves. Increase the heat and boil steadily, without stirring, until the sugar caramelizes (page 9). The temperature on a sugar thermometer will be 160°C/320°F. Lift the pan from the heat.
2. Have ready another 5 tablespoons cold water in a jug and pour it on to the sugar the moment it reaches the caramel stage. Swirl the pan, but do not stir (the mixture will sizzle and spit a little, so be careful) then continue to boil to a thick syrup, stirring to dissolve.
3. Meanwhile, beat the egg yolks in a bowl. Pour the hot caramel on to them, beating hard all the time, and continue beating until the mixture cools. Transfer the mixture to a freezer container.
4. Whip the cream until it forms soft peaks and fold it into the mixture with the walnuts. Freeze until firm without further stirring. F
F Freeze for 6 months.

CLOCKWISE FROM THE TOP: Pistachio ice cream; Pecan and maple syrup ice cream; Caramel walnut ice cream.

Eastern Promise

HALVA ICE CREAM

Serves 6-8
50 g (2 oz) butter
75 g (3 oz) semolina
25 g (1 oz) sesame seeds, toasted
1 teaspoon ground cinnamon
½ teaspoon ground cloves
50 g (2 oz) soft light brown sugar
250 ml (8 fl oz) water
100 g (4 oz) granulated sugar
2 eggs, separated
150 ml (¼ pint) double or whipping cream
fresh mint, to decorate

Preparation time: 15 minutes, plus cooling and freezing
Cooking time: 20 minutes

1. Melt the butter in a heavy saucepan, then stir in the semolina, sesame seeds, cinnamon and cloves and cook, stirring continuously, for about 5-6 minutes.
2. Lift the pan from the heat and stir in the brown sugar and half the water. Cook until the mixture thickens to a mass, cover the pan, turn off the heat and leave for 15 minutes for the semolina to swell. Allow to cool.
3. Place the granulated sugar and the remaining water in a heavy-based pan and boil to hard ball stage, 120°C/248°F on a sugar thermometer (page 9).
4. Put the egg whites in a medium bowl and beat until stiff. Pour on the boiling syrup in a thin stream, beating constantly, and continue beating hard until the mixture cools. Transfer the mixture to a freezer container.
5. Whip the cream until it forms soft peaks, then beat in the egg yolks and the cooled halva mixture. Fold into the meringue mixture and freeze until firm without further beating. F Decorate with fresh herbs.
F Freeze for 3 months.

Indian Summer

CARDAMOM ICE CREAM

Serves 6-8
6 cardamom pods
50 g (2 oz) granulated sugar
85 ml (3 fl oz) water
2 egg yolks
300 ml (½ pint) double or whipping cream
sprig of lemon verbena, to decorate

Preparation time: 20 minutes, plus freezing
Cooking time: 10 minutes

Cardamom is the second most expensive spice in the world (saffron is the most expensive). Its flavour is like a sweet version of eucalyptus; it rapidly loses its essential oils after it has been ground, so always buy it whole. Store in a screw-top jar in a cool, dark place.

1. Open the green cardamom pods, extract the seeds and crush them with a pestle in a mortar.
2. Place the sugar and water in a small heavy-based pan and stir over a low heat until dissolved, then, without stirring, boil until the syrup reaches thread stage,

Highland Fling

TOASTED OATMEAL ICE CREAM

Serves 6-8
600 ml (1 pint) milk
vanilla pod or 2-3 drops vanilla essence
5 egg yolks
100 g (4 oz) vanilla sugar
50 g (2 oz) medium oatmeal
50 g (2 oz) granulated sugar
300 ml (½ pint) double cream, chilled

Preparation time: 20 minutes, plus cooling and freezing
Cooking time: 20 minutes

This ice cream has a delicious nutty flavour. It is a variation of the classic old English favourite, brown bread ice cream.

1. Put the milk in a saucepan with the vanilla pod, if using, and bring just to boiling point.
2. Place the egg yolks and the sugar in a bowl and beat until pale and thick, then stir in the hot milk. Put the bowl over a pan of gently simmering water and, using a wooden spoon, continue to stir until the mixture thickens to a custard. Leave to cool.
3. Remove the vanilla pod or stir in the vanilla essence. Transfer the custard to a freezer container and freeze until the mixture is mushy.
4. Meanwhile, mix together the oatmeal and the granulated sugar on a flat flameproof tray and toast under a preheated grill, removing frequently to mix with a fork, until the sugar caramelizes. Break up with a fork into pieces the size of large crumbs, leave to cool, then chill in the refrigerator for 30 minutes.
5. Whip the cream to soft peaks. Beat the partially frozen custard, then fold in the caramelized oatmeal and the cream. Return to the freezer for another 1 hour, then beat once more to break up the crystals. Freeze until firm. ⑲
⑲ Freeze for 6 months.

107°C/225°F on a sugar thermometer (see page 9).
3. Put the egg yolks in a medium bowl and beat in the syrup, a little at a time, and continue beating hard until the mixture is thick and creamy.
4. In another bowl, whip the cream until it forms soft peaks, then fold it and the crushed cardamom seeds into the egg mousse.
5. Transfer the mixture to a freezer container and freeze until firm without further beating. ⑲ Serve in individual dishes, and decorate with fresh herbs.
⑲ Freeze for 6 months.

FROM THE LEFT: Cardamom ice cream; Halva ice cream.

Black Forest

CHOCOLATE AND BLACK CHERRY ICE CREAM

100 g (4 oz) plain chocolate, broken into pieces
1 tablespoon milk
1 × 175 g (6 oz) can evaporated milk, chilled
50 g (2 oz) icing sugar
2 tablespoons black cherry jam
fresh cherries, to decorate

Preparation time: *10 minutes, plus freezing*
Cooking time: *5 minutes*

1. Put the chocolate and the milk in the top of a double boiler or a heatproof bowl set over a pan of hot water and allow to melt gently.
2. Pour the evaporated milk into a medium bowl and whip until it forms soft peaks. Sift the icing sugar and whisk it in, then stir in the black cherry jam and the melted chocolate.
3. Transfer the mixture to a freezer container and freeze until firm without further beating. F Serve in individual glasses decorated with fresh cherries.
F Freeze for 3 months.

Sweet Dream

BUTTERSCOTCH ICE CREAM

50 g (2 oz) demerara sugar
85 ml (3 fl oz) water
75 g (3 oz) butter
2 egg yolks
300 ml (½ pint) double or whipping cream

Preparation time: *10 minutes, plus freezing*
Cooking time: *10 minutes*

1. Put the sugar and the water into a heavy-based pan and stir over a gentle heat until the sugar has dissolved, then boil without stirring until soft ball stage, 115°C/238°F on a sugar thermometer (page 9).
2. Add the butter and stir over a gentle heat until the butter melts and the mixture bubbles. Place the egg yolks in a medium bowl and beat in the buttery syrup, a little at a time, and continue beating hard until it is cool. Transfer to a freezer container.
3. Whip the cream until it forms soft peaks and fold it into the mixture. Freeze until firm without further beating. F Serve in wine glasses or individual glass dishes and decorate with fan biscuits or wafers.
F Freeze for 6 months.

Hidden Treasure

HAZELNUT AND CINNAMON ICE

3 tablespoons clear honey
300 ml (½ pint) water
2 × 5 cm (2 inch) sticks cinnamon
300 ml (½ pint) plain unsweetened yogurt, chilled
150 ml (¼ pint) double or whipping cream, chilled
100 g (4 oz) hazelnuts, chopped

Preparation time: *15 minutes, plus chilling and freezing*
Cooking time: *10 minutes*

1. Put the honey and the water in a heavy-based pan, add the cinnamon sticks and boil until the liquid is reduced by half. Allow to cool, then chill the mixture in the refrigerator.

2. Place the yogurt in a freezer container. Strain the honey mixture into the yogurt, stir, and freeze until mushy. This will take about 1½ hours.

3. Place the cream in a medium bowl and whip until it is stiff. Remove the semi-frozen mixture from the freezer, stir in the chopped hazelnuts and fold in the cream. Cover and freeze until firm, beating twice at hourly intervals. F Serve in individual glasses and top with whole hazelnuts, if liked.

F Freeze for 3 months.

FROM THE LEFT: Chocolate and black cherry ice cream; Butterscotch ice cream.

Crusoe's Choice

ICED COCONUT ICE

Serves 4-6
3 eggs, separated
175 g (6 oz) caster sugar
300 ml (½ pint) double or whipping cream
75 g (3 oz) desiccated coconut
1 teaspoon triple-strength rosewater (optional)
pink food colouring

Preparation time: 20 minutes, plus freezing

This ice cream is a particular favourite with children.

1. Line a 20 cm (8 inch) square tin with film.
2. In a large bowl whip the egg whites until stiff, then beat in the sugar, 1 teaspoon at a time.
3. Whip the cream until it forms soft peaks. Beat the egg yolks in another bowl and then stir in the desiccated coconut. Fold the cream into this mixture, then fold it all into the meringue mixture. Spread half the mixture into the lined tin.
4. Flavour the rest of the mixture with the rosewater, if liked, and colour it a delicate pink with food colouring, then spread it lightly on top of the white mixture and freeze until firm. F
5. To store, cover with another layer of film, or tip the ice out of the tin and wrap it in a freezer bag. To serve, unwrap the block and cut it into chunky slices or cubes. F Freeze for 6 months.

1. Put the milk and all but 2 tablespoons of the single cream into a saucepan with the vanilla pod if you are using one. Bring just to the boil. Remove from the heat.
2. Beat the eggs, yolks and sugar in a heatproof bowl until they are pale and thick, then pour on the boiling cream and milk, removing the vanilla pod if necessary.
3. Place the bowl over a pan of gently simmering water and stir until the custard is thick. Leave to cool, then chill in the refrigerator. Add the vanilla essence if using.
4. Whip the double cream until it forms soft peaks and fold it into the chilled custard. Transfer the mixture to a freezer container and freeze until firm, beating twice at hourly intervals to break up the crystals.
5. After the first beating, break the chocolate into pieces. Place it in the top of a double boiler with the remaining single cream and stir gently with a wooden spoon until the mixture is melted and smooth. Allow the mixture to cool without setting.
6. After the second beating, pour the melted chocolate into the ice cream and quickly stir it through the mixture with a fork. Freeze until firm. F
F Freeze for 6 months.

Marshmallow Rose

MARSHMALLOW ICE CREAM

Serves 4-6
120 g (4½ oz) packet pink and white marshmallows
150 ml (¼ pint) milk
150 ml (¼ pint) double or whipping cream
few drops, vanilla essence
25 g (1 oz) sieved icing sugar
1 egg white

Preparation time: *15 minutes, plus cooling and freezing*
Cooking time: *5 minutes*

1. Separate the pink and white marshmallows and place the white ones in a pan with the milk and melt them over a low heat, stirring all the time. Remove from the heat and leave to cool. Add the vanilla essence.
2. Beat the cream and whisk in the sugar. Turn into a freezer container and stir in the cooled white marshmallow mixture, cover and freeze until partially set.
3. Using scissors, cut up the pink marshmallows into small pieces. Beat the egg white until stiff. Remove the semi-frozen mixture from the freezer, and beat to combine the frozen and partially-frozen areas thoroughly. Fold in the pink marshmallow pieces and the egg white. Cover and freeze until firm. F
F Freeze for 3 months.

Chocolatapetl

VANILLA AND CHOCOLATE ICE CREAM

Serves 4-6
150 ml (¼ pint) milk
150 ml (¼ pint) single cream
vanilla pod or 2-3 drops vanilla essence
1 egg and 2 extra yolks
75 g (3 oz) vanilla sugar or caster sugar
150 ml (¼ pint) double or whipping cream
100 g (4 oz) plain chocolate

Preparation time: *20 minutes, plus chilling*
Cooking time: *20 minutes*

FROM THE LEFT: Iced coconut ice; Vanilla and chocolate ice cream; Marshmallow ice cream.

Sundaes, Sauces and Etceteras

Iced Lemon Soufflé

Serves 6
2 lemons
4 eggs, separated and 1 extra white
150 g (5 oz) caster sugar
300 ml (½ pint) double cream
lemon geranium leaves, to decorate

Preparation time: 20 minutes, plus freezing
Cooking time: 10 minutes

1. Prepare the 900 ml (1½ pint) soufflé dish. Tie a band of double thickness greaseproof paper or foil round the outside of the dish so that it stands 4 cm (1½ inches) above the rim.
2. Grate the rind finely from the lemons and put it in a small bowl. Squeeze the lemons and mix the juice with the lemon rind.
3. Place the egg yolks and 50 g (2 oz) of the sugar in a heatproof bowl set over a pan of boiling water, off the heat, and beat until pale and frothy. Beat in the lemon juice and rind.
4. Put the egg whites in a clean bowl and, using clean beaters, beat until they are frothy. Add the remaining sugar, 1 teaspoon at a time, beating hard all the time.
5. Whip the cream until it forms soft peaks and fold it into the yolk mixture, then fold in the meringue.
6. Turn the mixture into the prepared soufflé dish, smooth the surface and freeze for at least 4 hours until it is firm. 🄵
7. To serve, take the soufflé from the freezer, remove the collar, decorate the top with the scented geranium leaves and serve immediately.
🄵 Open freeze, then wrap in a polythene bag and freeze for up to 3 months.

Iced Coffee Rum Soufflé

Serves 6
4 eggs, separated, and 1 extra white
100 g (4 oz) caster sugar
2 tablespoons coffee essence
2 tablespoons rum
300 ml (½ pint) double cream
To finish:
3 tablespoons icing sugar
1 teaspoon instant coffee or coffee essence
flaked almonds
silver balls

Preparation time: 20 minutes, plus freezing

1. To prepare the 900 ml (1½ pint) soufflé dish, wrap a band of double thickness greaseproof paper or foil round the outside so that it stands 4 cm (1½ inches) above the rim. Fasten with string or a rubber band.
2. Put the egg yolks and 50 g (2 oz) caster sugar into a large bowl and whisk until pale and the consistency of lightly whipped cream. Whisk in the coffee essence and the rum. Whip the cream until it forms soft peaks and fold it into the egg yolk mixture.
3. Place the egg whites in another bowl and, using clean beaters, beat until they are frothy. Add the remaining caster sugar, 1 teaspoon at a time, continuing to beat hard until the mixture holds glossy peaks. Fold the egg whites into the yolk mixture and turn into the prepared soufflé dish and freeze for at least 4 hours until firm. 🄵
4. To serve, remove the collar from the soufflé dish. Place the icing sugar and the coffee flavouring in a jug and moisten with just enough hot water to give a pouring consistency. Trickle the sauce over the top of the soufflé and, using a palette knife, spread it lightly over the surface.
5. Decorate the top of the soufflé with 'flowers' of flaked almonds radiating from silver balls. Serve immediately. .
🄵 Open freeze, then wrap in a polythene bag and freeze for up to 3 months.

FROM THE LEFT: Iced lemon soufflé; Tropical glory.

Tropical Glory

½ recipe quantity Coffee ice cream (page 28)
½ recipe quantity Vanilla and chocolate ice cream (page 39)
Mocha Sauce:
3 tablespoons double or whipping cream
3 teaspoons sweetened coffee essence
4 squares dark chocolate
To decorate:
150 ml (¼ pint) double or whipping cream, whipped
25 g (1 oz) chopped nuts

Preparation time: 10 minutes, plus cooling and time for making the ice cream in advance
Cooking time: 2 minutes

1. Take the ice cream from the freezer 25-30 minutes before required and allow to soften in the refrigerator.
2. Chill 4 large tall glasses in the refrigerator for about 15 minutes.
3. Make the mocha sauce. Place the cream, the coffee essence and the chocolate in a small heavy-based saucepan and stir over a low heat until dissolved. Remove the pan from the heat and allow to cool.
4. Scoop the ice creams into the glasses in alternate layers until almost full.
5. Pour over the mocha sauce and decorate with the whipped cream and chopped nuts.

Iced Summer Pavlova

Serves 6
3 egg whites
150 g (5 oz) caster sugar
½ recipe quantity Raspberry and redcurrant
  ice cream (page 18)
Strawberry Curaçao Ice Cream:
350 g (12 oz) strawberries
100 g (4 oz) icing sugar
3 tablespoons Orange Curaçao
300 ml (½ pint) double cream, chilled
To decorate:
150 ml (¼ pint) double or whipping cream
1 kiwi fruit, peeled and sliced
a few strawberries or raspberries

Preparation time: *35 minutes, plus freezing and cooling*
Cooking time: *2-2½ hours*
Oven: *140°C, 275°F, Gas Mark 1 then: 120°C, 250°F, Gas Mark ½*

Pavlova is Australia's most famous dessert. It was named in honour of the great Russian ballerina. The light meringue base is built up at the sides to simulate a dancer's tutu.

1. Make the strawberry Curaçao ice cream. Liquidize the strawberries to a purée or rub through a nylon sieve with a wooden spoon. Stir in the icing sugar and the Curaçao. Transfer the mixture to a freezer container and freeze for about 1 hour until firm round the edges.
2. Whip the cream until it holds soft peaks. Remove the strawberry ice from the freezer and beat until smooth. Fold the cream into the strawberry ice and freeze until firm, beating once more after another 1 hour. F
3. Line a large lightly greased baking sheet with non-stick silicone paper or lightly greased greaseproof paper.
4. Place the egg whites in a large bowl and whisk them until they stand in stiff peaks. Gradually beat in the sugar, a little at a time, whisking well after each addition, until the mixture is thick and glossy.
5. Pipe or spread the meringue in a wide circle on the baking sheet, starting in the centre and coiling the mixture round on itself. Pipe an extra layer, like a wall, round the edge of the meringue. Bake in a preheated oven for about 30 minutes or until the meringue is tinged with gold. Reduce the oven temperature and bake for a further 1½-2 hours. Leave the meringue to cool in the oven to prevent cracking. A F
6. About 30 minutes before serving, transfer the raspberry and redcurrant ice cream and the strawberry Curaçao ice cream to the refrigerator to soften.
7. Carefully transfer the meringue case to a large flat dish. Using an ice cream scoop, fill the case with balls of each ice cream alternately. Whip the cream until it holds soft peaks and swirl it on top of the ice cream. Decorate with slices of kiwi fruit and raspberries or strawberries.
A Make the meringue case 2 days ahead and store in an airtight tin.
F Pack the meringue case in a rigid container and freeze for 3 months. Thaw for 1 hour at room temperature.
F Freeze the strawberry Curaçao ice cream for 3 months.

Melon Split

2 small Galia or Ogen melons, chilled
4 tablespoons ginger wine (optional)
Ginger Ice Cream:
50 g (2 oz) granulated sugar
85 ml (3 oz) water
2 egg yolks
2 tablespoons preserved ginger, finely chopped
1 tablespoon syrup from the ginger
300 ml (½ pint) double or whipping cream, chilled

Preparation time: *15 minutes, plus freezing*
Cooking time: *10 minutes*

1. Make the ginger ice cream. Put the sugar and the water in a small heavy-based saucepan and stir over a low heat until the sugar dissolves. Bring the syrup to the boil and boil, without stirring, until it reaches thread stage, 107°C/225°F on a sugar thermometer (page 9).
2. Put the egg yolks in a medium bowl and beat in the syrup, a little at a time, continuing to beat until the mixture is cool. Stir in the ginger and the ginger syrup.
3. Whip the cream in a bowl until it forms soft peaks, then fold it into the ginger mixture. Transfer the mixture to a freezer container and freeze until firm without further beating. F
4. Remove the ice cream from the freezer 25-30 minutes before it is required and leave it to soften in the refrigerator. Chill the melons in the refrigerator.
5. Cut the melons in half with zigzag cuts, scoop out the seeds and discard them. Scoop ice cream into the middle of each melon half and dribble ginger wine over, if using. Serve immediately.
F Freeze for 6 months.

FROM THE TOP: Melon split; Iced summer pavlova.

Chocolate Fudge Sundae

Serves 6
1 recipe quantity Vanilla and chocolate ice cream (page 39)
1 recipe quantity Fudge sauce (page 56)
150 ml (¼ pint) whipping cream
50 g (2 oz) chopped nuts
25 g (1 oz) chocolate vermicelli
6 milk chocolate flakes

Preparation time: *10 minutes, plus softening and freezing or time for making the ice cream in advance*

The ice cream for this recipe needs to be frozen in a specially shaped container. Therefore time should be allowed for making it in advance, or, if it is already in the freezer, for softening it in the refrigerator until it can be pressed into the appropriate container.

1. After its second beating or after it has softened, transfer the ice cream to a square tray, cover and return to the freezer. Freeze until firm.
2. Remove the ice cream from the freezer and allow it to soften in the refrigerator for 20 minutes before serving.
3. Chill 6 dishes in the refrigerator for 15 minutes.
4. Slice the ice cream into 2.5 cm (1 inch) cubes and arrange in piles on the individual dishes, pour on the cooled fudge sauce, and decorate each portion with the whipped cream, a scattering of nuts and chocolate vermicelli and a chocolate flake.

Danish Delight

Serves 6
100 g (4 oz) butter
275 g (10 oz) fresh white breadcrumbs
1 recipe quantity Apple butter ice cream (page 17)
150 ml (¼ pint) whipping cream, whipped
75 g (3 oz) dark chocolate, grated

Preparation time: *10 minutes, plus chilling*
Cooking time: *10 minutes*

This sundae is inspired by a traditional Danish dessert known as veiled peasant girl, veiled country lass and other similar names. It is made with layers of stewed apple or apple sauce and the toasted breadcrumbs are often made from pumpernickel or very dark rye bread. Like this luscious summer variation, it is generally topped with whipped cream and grated chocolate.

1. Melt the butter in a frying pan and fry the breadcrumbs, stirring and turning until crisp. Remove the breadcrumbs from the pan and drain them on crumpled paper towels. Leave to cool.
2. Transfer the apple butter ice cream to the refrigerator and allow to soften for 15 minutes. Chill 6 tall stemmed glasses in the refrigerator for 15 minutes.
3. Spoon alternate layers of fried crumbs and ice cream into the chilled glasses. Top each glass with a swirl of whipped cream and a spoonful of grated chocolate.

Only whipping and double cream can be whipped successfully, and the best results are obtained if the cream is chilled in the refrigerator first. It helps too, particularly in hot weather, if the bowl and beaters are chilled for 20-30 minutes before using. Whipping cream should whip to twice its original bulk, and double cream can be made to go further and give a lighter and airier finish if it is whipped with the same quantity of single cream (transforming it into whipping cream) or using 1-2 tablespoons of iced water to every half pint of cream. Whipped cream deflates on contact with anything warm, so make sure that anything to be folded into it is chilled as well.

FROM THE LEFT: Chocolate fudge sundae; Danish delight.

Banana Coffee Split Flambé

Serves 2
3 small ripe bananas
½ recipe quantity Coffee ice cream (page 28)
4 tablespoons whipped cream
4 tablespoons Sambuca
6 whole coffee beans

Preparation time: 5 minutes, plus softening and making the ice cream

Sambuca is an Italian aniseed flavoured liqueur. In Italy it is sometimes served *"con mosche"* ("with flies") i.e. coffee beans floating on the surface. The Sambuca is ignited which burns off the alcohol at the same time as roasting the beans. This is an elaborate iced version.

1. Remove the ice cream from the freezer 30 minutes before it is required and allow it to soften in the refrigerator.
2. Peel the bananas, then cut them in half and split each half lengthways.
3. Scoop the ice cream into heatproof dishes and arrange a barricade of banana around each portion. Spoon whipped cream on top of the ice cream.
4. Run a moat of Sambuca round the barricades of banana and scatter 3 coffee beans in each moat. Set light to the Sambuca and serve immediately.

Shattered Blackcurrant Meringue

Serves 6-8
750 g (1½ lb) blackcurrants
50 g (2 oz) caster sugar
50 g (2 oz) granulated sugar
85 ml (3 fl oz) water
2 egg yolks
300 ml (½ pint) double cream
Meringue:
2 egg whites
100 g (4 oz) caster sugar

Preparation time: 30 minutes, plus freezing and softening
Cooking time: about 1 hour

1. Put the blackcurrants and the caster sugar in a saucepan and simmer until the juice runs. Rub the fruit through a sieve to remove the pips and leave to cool.
2. Place the granulated sugar and the water in a small heavy-based saucepan and stir well over a low heat until the sugar dissolves. Bring to the boil, without stirring, and boil to thread stage, 107°C/225°F on a sugar thermometer (page 9).
3. Put the egg yolks in a medium bowl and beat in the sugar syrup, a little at a time, and continue to beat until the mixture is cool.
4. Whip the cream until it holds soft peaks and fold it into the egg mixture with half the blackcurrant purée. Turn into a freezer container and freeze until firm. Chill the remaining purée in the refrigerator. ⒡
5. Line 2 lightly greased baking sheets with non-stick silicone paper or lightly greased greaseproof paper.
6. Make the meringue. Put the egg whites in a bowl and beat them until they hold peaks. Beat in 50 g (2 oz) of the caster sugar, one third at a time, beating between each addition. Carefully fold in the remaining sugar.
7. Using a metal dessert spoon, spoon out small swirls of meringue on to the prepared baking sheets and bake in a preheated oven for about 1 hour until just crisp. ⒜ ⒡ Reserve 8 meringues for decoration and roughly crush the rest.
8. Transfer the ice cream to the refrigerator for 15-20 minutes to soften. Chill a large serving dish.
9. To serve, fold the crushed meringue into the ice cream and pile on to the chilled serving dish. Spoon the reserved blackcurrant purée over and decorate with the reserved meringues.

⒜ Make the meringues 2-4 days in advance and store in an airtight tin.
⒡ The blackcurrant purée can be frozen for 3 months. Thaw overnight in the refrigerator. Pack the meringues in rigid containers sand freeze for 3 months. Thaw at room temperature for 1 hour.

FROM THE LEFT: Banana coffee split flambé; Shattered blackcurrant meringue.

Sticky Brown Meringue Glacé

Serves 6
2 egg whites
100 g (4 oz) soft light brown sugar
1 recipe quantity Toffee apple ice cream (page 25)
apple slices, to decorate

Preparation time: *15 minutes, plus cooling and softening*
Cooking time: *1 hour*
Oven: *140°C, 275°F, Gas Mark 1*

1. Put the egg whites in a bowl and beat them until they hold soft peaks. Beat in 50 g (2 oz) of the sugar, one third at a time, beating between each addition so that the mixture becomes thick and glossy. Mix in the remaining sugar all at once with as little beating as possible.
2. Line a lightly greased baking sheet with non-stick silicone paper or lightly greased greaseproof paper. Pipe or spoon out the meringue mixture into twelve rounds and bake in a preheated oven for 1 hour.
3. Carefully remove the meringues from the paper with a palette knife and leave to cool on a wire tray. Ⓐ Ⓕ
4. Take the ice cream from the freezer 25-30 minutes before it is required and allow it to soften in the refrigerator.
5. Sandwich the meringues together with scoops of ice cream and decorate with slices of apple.
Ⓐ The meringues can be prepared up to 2 weeks in advance and stored in an airtight tin.
Ⓕ Pack the meringues in rigid containers and freeze for up to 3 months. Thaw at room temperature for 1 hour.

Mocha Alaska

Serves 8
1 recipe quantity Vanilla and chocolate ice cream (page 39)
100 g (4 oz) granulated sugar
150 ml (¼ pint) water
2 egg whites
1 tablespoon sweetened coffee essence
1 × 20 cm (8 inch) chocolate Victoria sponge

Preparation time: *20 minutes, plus freezing and softening or time for making the ice cream in advance*
Cooking time: *15 minutes*
Oven: *240°C, 475°F, Gas Mark 9*

When making an alaska, it is essential that the meringue covers the ice cream and the sponge completely without leaving any gaps.

1. Freeze the ice cream after its second beating, or, after softening, transfer it to a plastic, metal or foil bowl with a top diameter of not more than 18 cm (7 inches). Return to the freezer.
2. Put the sugar and water in a small heavy-based saucepan and stir over a low heat until the sugar dissolves. Bring to the boil, without stirring, and boil to hard ball stage, 120°C/248°F on a sugar thermometer (page 9).
3. Meanwhile, beat the egg whites in a bowl until they are stiff. Pour the boiling syrup on to the egg whites in a thin stream, beating hard, and continue to beat hard until the mixture is cool. Beat in the coffee essence. Ⓐ
4. To assemble the alaska, place the Victoria sponge on a flat ovenproof dish. Wipe the ice cream mould with tea towels rinsed out in hot water to loosen the ice cream then turn out the ice cream on to the centre of the sponge. Using a palette knife, liberally swathe the ice cream and the sponge in meringue, making sure it covers thickly and meets the serving dish all round. Bake for 3 minutes in a preheated oven and serve immediately.
Ⓐ The meringue mixture can be made a few hours ahead and kept covered, in the refrigerator.

FROM THE TOP: Mocha alaska; Sticky brown meringue glacé.

Iced Peach Condé

Serves 6
400 g (14 oz) can creamed rice
150 ml (¼ pint) double or whipping cream
25 g (1 oz) caster sugar
450 g (1 lb) fresh or frozen strawberries, thawed
100 g (4 oz) icing sugar
1 teaspoon arrowroot
2 teaspoons lemon juice
3 large ripe peaches, skinned, stoned and sliced
whipped cream, to serve

Preparation time: *20 minutes, plus freezing and softening*

1. Put the creamed rice in a blender and purée until smooth. Spoon the purée into a freezer container and freeze, beating twice at hourly intervals so that the mixture freezes evenly.
2. Place the cream in a bowl with the caster sugar and whisk until it forms soft peaks. Fold the cream into the rice after the second beating. Return the mixture to the freezer and freeze until firm. F
3. Make the sauce. Rub the strawberries through a sieve into a bowl. Beat in the icing sugar, 1 tablespoon at a time. Mix together the arrowroot and the lemon juice. Place in a saucepan. Pour in the strawberry purée and heat gently, stirring continuously until the mixture thickens. Chill in the refrigerator. A
4. Transfer the iced rice from the freezer to the refrigerator 30-40 minutes before required.
5. Put 6 individual dishes in the refrigerator to chill 15 minutes before required.
6. To serve, scoop the rice into the chilled dishes, top with peach slices and pour on the sauce. Serve immediately with whipped cream.
A Can be made the day before and chilled until required.
F The rice mixture can be frozen for up to 6 months.

Atholl Brose Parfait

Serves 6-8
1 recipe quantity Toasted oatmeal ice cream (page 35)
3 tablespoons clear honey
3 tablespoons whisky
450 g (1 lb) raspberries, fresh or thawed

Preparation time: *5 minutes, plus softening and freezing or time for making the ice cream in advance*
Cooking time: *2 minutes*

The ice cream for this recipe needs to be frozen in a specially shaped container. Therefore time should be allowed for making it in advance, or, if it is already in the freezer, for softening it for 25-30 minutes in the refrigerator until it can be pressed into the appropriate container.

1. Place the toasted oatmeal ice cream in a 1.5 litre (2½ pint) ring mould after the last beating or after softening. Freeze until firm.
2. Make a sauce by placing the honey and the whisky in a small saucepan and stirring over a low heat until they amalgamate. Remove the pan from the heat and leave the mixture to cool.
3. To serve, take the ring mould from the freezer and run a thin knife round the inner and outer edges of the mould. Invert the mould on to a chilled serving plate and press a tea towel wrung out in hot water on to the top of the mould for 30 seconds. Lift the mould from the ice cream. Fill the centre of the mould with the raspberries and trickle the whisky sauce over the ice cream.

FROM THE TOP: Atholl brose parfait; Iced peach condé.

Black Forest Bombe

Serves 8
1 quantity Chocolate ice cream (see below)
50 g (2 oz) granulated sugar
85 ml (3 fl oz) water
2 egg yolks
50 g (2 oz) maraschino cherries, coarsely chopped
1 tablespoon syrup from maraschino cherries
2 tablespoons cherry brandy
300 ml (½ pint) double or whipping cream, chilled
To decorate:
whipped cream
maraschino cherries

Preparation time: 20 minutes, plus softening, freezing and chilling
Cooking time: 10 minutes

1. To make the chocolate ice cream, follow the recipe for Vanilla and chocolate ice cream (page 39) but first melt the chocolate in the milk to be used for the custard. Freeze the chocolate ice cream until firm.
2. Chill a 1.5 litre (2½ pint) bombe mould in the freezer for at least 30 minutes.
3. Take the chocolate ice cream out of the freezer and allow to soften for 25-30 minutes at room temperature. Line the base and sides of the mould evenly with the chocolate ice cream. Return the mould to the freezer straightaway and freeze until firm.
4. Place the sugar and the water in a small heavy-based saucepan over a low heat and stir until the sugar dissolves completely. Bring to the boil and then boil, without stirring, to thread stage, 107°C/225°F on a sugar thermometer (page 9).
5. Beat the egg yolks in a medium bowl. Pour the syrup on to them, a little at a time, beating hard continually until the mixture cools.
6. Stir the chopped cherries, their syrup and the cherry brandy into the egg mixture. Whip the cream until it forms soft peaks and fold it into the mixture. Chill the mixture in the refrigerator for 1 hour.
7. Take the bombe mould from the freezer and spoon the chilled mixture into the frozen ice cream shell. Cover the bombe and freeze for several hours, preferably overnight. F
8. About 15-30 minutes before it is required, transfer the bombe mould from the freezer to the refrigerator.
9. To remove the bombe from the mould, remove the lid and invert the mould on to a chilled serving plate. Wrap a clean tea towel, wrung out in hot water, round the mould for 30 seconds. Gently ease the mould away from the ice cream.
10. Decorate the bombe with whipped cream, and maraschino cherries.
F Can be frozen for 3 months.

Jamaica Bombe

Serves 8
50 g (2 oz) seedless raisins
3 tablespoons rum
1 recipe quantity Coffee ice cream (page 28)
50 g (2 oz) granulated sugar
85 ml (3 fl oz) water
2 egg yolks
300 ml (½ pint) double cream, chilled
To decorate:
150 ml (¼ pint) double cream
crystallized violets

Preparation time: 20 minutes, plus soaking, softening and freezing
Cooking time: 10 minutes

1. Put the raisins in a bowl and spoon the rum over. Leave to macerate overnight.
2. Place a 1.5 litre (2½ pint) bombe mould in the freezer and chill for at least 30 minutes.
3. Remove the coffee ice cream from the freezer and allow to soften for 20-30 minutes at room temperature. Line the base and sides of the mould with the coffee ice cream to give an even layer. Return the mould to the freezer immediately and freeze until firm.
4. Place the sugar and the water in a small heavy-based pan and stir over a low heat until the sugar dissolves. Bring the syrup to the boil and boil without stirring until it reaches thread stage, 107°C/225°F on a sugar thermometer (page 9).
5. Beat the egg yolks into a bowl. Pour the syrup on to the egg yolks, a little at a time, beating hard all the time. Continue beating until the mixture is cool. Stir in the raisins and rum.
6. Place the cream in a bowl and whip it until it forms soft peaks, then fold it into the mixture. Chill the mixture in the refrigerator for 1 hour.
7. Take the bombe mould from the freezer and spoon the chilled mixture into the frozen ice cream shell. Cover and freeze preferably, overnight. F
8. About 15-30 minutes before it is required, transfer the bombe mould from the freezer to the refrigerator.
9. To remove the bombe from the mould, remove the lid and invert the mould on to a chilled serving plate. Wrap a clean teatowel wrung out in hot water, round the mould for 30 seconds. Gently ease the mould away from the ice cream.
10. Whip the double cream until stiff and pipe a border round the bombe and decorate it with the crystallized violets.
F Can be frozen for 3 months.

FROM THE TOP: Black Forest bombe; Jamaica bombe.

Thick Chocolate Sauce

2 teaspoons cornflour
150 ml (¼ pint) milk
6 squares (about 25 g (1 oz)) dark chocolate
2 tablespoons double or whipping cream

Preparation time: 2 minutes
Cooking time: 10 minutes

A beautiful sauce to serve with coffee ice cream and all sorts of fruit based ice creams.

1. Spoon the cornflour into a mixed bowl and blend to a cream with 1 tablespoon of the milk. Pour the remaining milk into a pan, add the chocolate squares and stir gently over a low heat until the chocolate melts.
2. Stir the chocolate milk into the cornflour, a little at a time, so that it blends in smoothly, then return it to the rinsed pan. Stir in the cream, place the pan over a low heat, stirring all the time, until the sauce is thick and smooth. Serve immediately, to prevent the sauce forming a skin.

Spicy Fruit Topping

Serves 4-6
350 g (12 oz) mixed dried apricots, peaches, apples or pears (in any combination of two or more)
100 g (4 oz) raisins
100 g (4 oz) sultanas
2 × 5 cm (2 inch) sticks of cinnamon
4 cloves
2 inch strip of lemon peel
4 tablespoons clear honey
4 tablespoons rum

Preparation time: 15 minutes, plus soaking
Cooking time: 10 minutes

A sauce with a Middle Eastern flavour. Serve it with vanilla ice cream, apple or spiced ices.

1. Soak all the fruit overnight, or for at least 4 hours, in cold water to cover, with the cinnamon, cloves and lemon peel. Drain, reserving 4 tablespoons of the soaking liquor.
2. Chop the large fruit coarsely, then put it into a pan with the raisins, sultanas, spices and peel, the reserved soaking liquor, the honey and the rum. Simmer for 10 minutes, then allow to cool. Ⓐ Chill in the refrigerator and serve cold.
Ⓐ Store for up to 1 year in screw-top jars in a cool dry place.

Cherry Jubilee Sauce

Serves 6
450 g (1 lb) red cherries
150 g (5 oz) granulated sugar
thinly peeled rind of ½ lemon
1 tablespoon lemon juice
300 ml (½ pint) water
1 tablespoon cornflour
4 tablespoons cherry brandy

Preparation time: 10 minutes
Cooking time: 25 minutes

Serve this sauce hot on vanilla, chocolate or nut ices. For high drama, spoon it hot over hard-frozen ice cream, then warm the brandy, pour it over and set fire to it, so what arrives at table is a spectacular combination of fire and ice.

1. Stone the cherries and put the stones, stems and sugar in a heavy-based pan with the lemon rind and juice. Pour on the water and stir over a low heat until the sugar dissolves, then bring to the boil and let it simmer for 10 minutes.
2. Strain the syrup into a clean pan and add the cherries. Simmer for 3 minutes Ⓕ, then mix the cornflour to a thin paste with a little cold water. Pour it on to the cherries in a thin stream, stirring constantly, and simmer until the sauce thickens and becomes clear.
3. Stir in the cherry brandy, pour the sauce into a jug and serve immediately. Ⓐ
Ⓐ Can be kept in a covered container in the refrigerator for 1 week.
Ⓕ Pack the cherries with their syrup in a rigid container with 1-2 cm (½-1 inch) headspace and freeze for 3 months. Thaw at room temperature for 4 hours.

CLOCKWISE FROM THE TOP: Thick chocolate sauce; Cherry jubilee sauce; Spicy fruit topping.

Fudge Sauce

Serves 4-6
75 g (3 oz) butter
1 tablespoon golden syrup
75 g (3 oz) brown sugar
4 tablespoons evaporated milk

Cooking time: 10 minutes

Serve this sauce with apricot ice cream or use it to liven up a plain vanilla. It is equally good hot, warm or cold.

1. Place all the ingredients in a heavy-based pan and heat gently until the sugar has dissolved, stirring all the time with a wooden spoon.
2. Bring to the boil, then remove the pan from the heat. Serve immediately or allow to cool. Ⓐ
Ⓐ This sauce can be made in advance and stored in the refrigerator in a covered container for 3-4 days.

A sauce to make in quantity when raspberries are cheap or profuse in the garden. It will dress a year's worth of sundaes or knickerbocker glories in classic ice cream parlour style. Don't confuse this sweetened raspberry vinegar with the unsweetened version which is so popular in nouvelle cuisine. This one is definitely for dessert use only.

1. Put the raspberries and the vinegar in a glass or china bowl and leave to stand, covered, for 3-4 days.
2. Line a sieve with a folded muslin cloth, place over a preserving pan and strain the raspberry liquid (or use a jelly bag). Do not squeeze or crush the fruit or the vinegar will be cloudy.
3. Add 450 g (1 lb) sugar for each 600 ml (1 pint) liquid. Stir over the heat until the sugar dissolves, then boil for 10 minutes, leave to cool for a few minutes, then pour into sterilized bottles. Ⓐ
Ⓐ Store for up to 1 year in a cool larder.

Chocolate Caramel Sauce

2 chocolate coated nougat and caramel bars
4 tablespoons evaporated milk

Preparation time: 2 minutes
Cooking time: 3 minutes

1. Slice the chocolate bars thinly, then put them in a small heavy-based pan with 3½ tablespoons of the evaporated milk and melt over a gentle heat stirring continuously.
2. Serve warm with vanilla ice cream. Decorate with the remaining evaporated milk swirled through the sauce.

Sweet Raspberry Vinegar

Makes 1 litre (1¾ pints)
900 g (2 lb) raspberries
1 litre (1¾ pints) red or white wine vinegar
700 g (about 1½ lb) caster sugar

Preparation time: 10 minutes, plus 3-4 days standing
Cooking time: 15 minutes

FROM THE LEFT: Fudge sauce; Sweet raspberry vinegar; Chocolate caramel sauce.

Honey Curls

Makes 14
150 g (5 oz) caster sugar
50 g (2 oz) butter
50 g (2 oz) clear honey
50 g (2 oz) plain flour
½ teaspoon ground cinnamon

Preparation time: 15 minutes
Cooking time: 15 minutes
Oven: 180°C, 350°F, Gas Mark 4

1. Weigh out the sugar, butter and honey together so that the sugar prevents the honey sticking, and put them into a heavy-based pan. Stir together over a low heat until the butter and sugar melt. Remove the pan from the heat.
2. Sift the flour and cinnamon into a bowl and mix them lightly into the honey mixture. Place 3 teaspoonfuls of the mixture, well apart, on lightly greased baking trays (3 honey curls to each baking sheet) and bake for 7-10 minutes until golden. Do not prepare more than 3 trays of honey curls at a time.
3. Using a palette knife, remove the biscuits from the baking sheets as quickly as you can and curl each one round the handle of a wooden spoon. Leave for 1-2 minutes to set, then slip off carefully on to wire trays to cool. Ⓐ
Ⓐ Can be made the day before and stored in an airtight tin.

Sand Biscuits

Makes 20-30 depending on the size of the cutter
225 g (8 oz) plain flour
90 g (3½ oz) granulated sugar, and a little more to finish
½ teaspoon salt
100 g (4 oz) butter
1 egg and 1 extra yolk

Preparation time: 20 minutes, plus cooling
Cooking time: 8-10 minutes
Oven: 180°C, 350°F, Gas Mark 4

The gritty texture and buttery taste of these little biscuits goes well with most creamy ices.

1. Mix the flour, sugar and salt in a bowl. Rub in the butter to make a crumbly mixture.
2. Beat the egg and yolk together with a fork. Make a well in the middle of the mixture, pour in the eggs and mix to a dough, first with a fork and then with your hands. Knead into a ball in the bowl, then chill in the refrigerator for 30 minutes.
3. Grease 2 baking trays. Roll out the dough to 5 mm (¾ inch) thick on a floured board with a floured rolling pin. Using a shaped or fluted cutter cut out biscuits and arrange in rows on the baking trays.
4. Scatter lightly with a little granulated sugar and bake 8-10 minutes in a preheated oven until they are crisp and tinged with gold around the edges. Cool on a wire tray. Ⓐ
Ⓐ Can be kept for 2 days in an airtight tin.

Hazelnut Thins

Makes about 60 biscuits
75 g (3 oz) shelled hazelnuts
100 g (4 oz) butter
225 g (8 oz) soft brown sugar
1 egg
200 g (7 oz) plain flour
pinch of salt
½ teaspoon bicarbonate of soda

Preparation time: 20 minutes, plus chilling overnight
Cooking time: 12-15 minutes
Oven: 180°C, 350°F, Gas Mark 4

1. Spread the hazelnuts on a baking sheet and toast under a preheated grill, shaking frequently. When the brown skins look loose and flaky, cool the nuts until you can handle them, then rub handfuls between your hands to slough off the skins. Chop the nuts finely.
2. Cream the butter and sugar in a mixing bowl. Beat in the egg, then stir in the nuts.
3. Sift the flour, salt and bicarbonate of soda together and mix in.
4. Form the dough into a cylinder and chill overnight in the refrigerator. Ⓕ
5. Slice the biscuits thinly from the cylinder and prick with a fork. Place on a lightly greased baking sheet and bake in a preheated oven for about 8 minutes.
Ⓕ The cylinder of dough can be wrapped in freezer film and stored for 6 months in the freezer. It can then be sliced and baked from frozen while your ice cream is softening in the refrigerator.

TOP LEFT: Honey curls; top right; Sand biscuits; bottom: Hazelnut thins.

Fruit Flourishes

Baked Nectarines

Serves 6
6 large ripe nectarines
4 almond macaroons, crushed
50 g (2 oz) mixed glacé fruits, finely shredded
½ egg, beaten
25 g (1 oz) butter
150 ml (¼ pint) sweet white wine or sweet sherry

Preparation time: *5 minutes*
Cooking time: *20-30 minutes*
Oven: *200°C, 400°F, Gas Mark 6*

1. Wash the nectarines and halve them.
2. Remove the stones. Using a teaspoon, scrape out a little of the flesh to enlarge the cavity slightly.
3. Put the extra pulp into a bowl and mix with the crushed macaroons, glacé fruits and the beaten egg.
4. Fill the nectarine cavities with the mixture.
5. Using 15 g (½ oz) of the butter, lightly grease a shallow dish large enough to hold the nectarine halves in a single layer.
6. Place the halves stuffing side up. Dot each one with a little of the remaining butter and sprinkle with the wine.
7. Bake in a preheated oven for 20-30 minutes until tender and serve hot with whipped cream.

Red and Black Compote

Serves 8
225 g (8 oz) sugar
300 ml (½ pint) water
450 g (1 lb) redcurrants
450 g (1 lb) blackcurrants
1 tablespoon arrowroot
juice of ½ lemon

Preparation time: *5 minutes, plus cooling*
Cooking time: *25 minutes*

1. Dissolve the sugar and water in a medium pan over a gentle heat.
2. Bring to the boil, then add the fruit and simmer gently for 15 minutes.

3. Strain the fruit, reserving the liquor and spoon the fruit into a serving dish.
4. Return the syrup to the pan and bring it to the boil. Blend the arrowroot with the lemon juice. Remove the saucepan from the heat and stir in the arrowroot.
5. Return the pan to the heat, stirring until the syrup is thick and clear. Pour the syrup over the fruit. Cool before serving. Ⓐ
Ⓐ Can be prepared the previous day, covered tightly with clingfilm and kept chilled.

Glazed Peaches

4 peaches
juice of 1 lemon
300 ml (½ pint) red wine
100 g (4 oz) caster sugar
1 cinnamon stick
herb leaves, to decorate

Preparation time: *10 minutes, plus cooling*
Cooking time: *35 minutes*

1. Dip the peaches into boiling water for 20 seconds, then put them into iced water to stop them cooking.
2. Carefully peel the peaches and rub a little lemon juice over them to prevent discoloration.
3. Put the wine, sugar and cinnamon stick in a heavy-based saucepan and bring to the boil, stirring all the time until the sugar has dissolved.
4. Lower the heat and place the peaches in the wine syrup. Poach for about 30 minutes until they are tender, turning them occasionally. Ⓕ
5. Remove the peaches from the syrup with a slotted spoon and place in a serving dish.
6. Boil the syrup fiercely until it is thick enough to coat the peaches. Spoon the syrup over the peaches and leave to cool. Serve in individual dishes and decorate each peach with a herb leaf.
Ⓕ Pack into a rigid container and freeze for up to 6 months. Thaw in the container at room temperature for 3-4 hours.

CLOCKWISE FROM TOP LEFT: Glazed peaches; Red and black compote; Tipsy strawberries.

Tipsy Strawberries

750 g (1½ lb) strawberries, hulled
100 g (4 oz) caster sugar
50 ml (2 fl oz) Curaçao
25 ml (1 fl oz) port

Preparation time: 10 minutes, plus chilling

For a change try using Cointreau or Grand Marnier in place of the Curaçao.

1. Roll the strawberries in sugar. Arrange them in a serving dish or individual glasses and pour over the Curaçao and port.
2. Chill well for 1 hour. Decorate with strawberry leaves or wild strawberries, if available, and serve with cream and Sand biscuits (page 59).

Exotic Fruit Medley

Serves 6-8
1 large pineapple
2 passion fruit
2 kiwi fruit, peeled and sliced
1 mango, peeled and sliced, stone removed
3 tablespoons Kirsch

Preparation time: 30 minutes, plus cooling

1. Cut off the top of the pineapple and reserve.
2. Cut out the flesh of the pineapple by cutting round it with a long sharp knife and scooping out the flesh with a metal spoon.
3. Slice the flesh into bite-sized pieces, discarding the hard core.
4. Halve the passion fruit and spoon out the flesh.
5. Mix all the fruits together in a bowl with the Kirsch. Spoon them into the pineapple shell and chill.
6. Just before serving, replace the pineapple top. Serve with plain unsweetened yogurt or a pouring cream.

Gooseberry Cream

450 g (1 lb) gooseberries, topped and tailed
3 tablespoons water
100 g (4 oz) caster sugar
300 ml (½ pint) double or whipping cream
few drops green food colouring (optional)
frosted primroses, to decorate (see box right)

Preparation time: 10 minutes, plus cooling and chilling
Cooking time: 15 minutes

Vary the flavour of this traditional English dessert by adding a little orange flower water with the cream or cooking an elderflower head (tie it in a piece of muslin first) with the gooseberries.

1. Place the gooseberries in a saucepan with the water, bring to the boil, then simmer gently for 15 minutes or until soft. Sieve into a bowl, stir in the sugar and leave to cool for about 30 minutes. Ⓐ Ⓕ
2. Whip the cream until it forms soft peaks, then fold into the gooseberry purée. Spoon into individual glasses and chill until required. Decorate before serving.
Ⓐ The purée can be prepared up to 24 hours in advance and kept, covered, in the refrigerator.
Ⓕ Freeze the purée in a rigid container with 1 cm (½ inch) headspace for up to 6 months. Thaw overnight in the refrigerator.

Orange and Grapefruit Special

Serves 8
4 seedless oranges
4 grapefruits
225 g (8 oz) sugar
250 ml (8 fl oz) water
3 tablespoons Grand Marnier

Preparation time: 15 minutes, plus chilling
Cooking time: 25 minutes

1. With a sharp knife or vegetable peeler, pare the rind from 1 orange and half a grapefruit and shred finely.
2. Put the rind in a small pan and cover with boiling water. Bring to the boil and simmer for 2 minutes then drain carefully.
3. Using a sharp knife peel the oranges and grapefruits, removing all the pith.
4. Separate the fruit into segments, cutting the larger ones in half, and arrange them in a serving dish.
5. Put the sugar and 120 ml (4 fl oz) of the water into a heavy saucepan. Heat gently, stirring all the time, without letting it boil until all the sugar has dissolved.
6. Increase the heat and boil until it is a rich golden caramel. This will register 168°C/336°F on a sugar thermometer (page 9).
7. Meanwhile bring the remaining water to the boil in a saucepan. Remove the caramel from the heat and quickly pour in the hot water. Take great care as the water will splutter over the pan.
8. Stir until the caramel has melted, returning to the heat briefly if necessary. Leave to cool. Add the Grand Marnier.
9. Sprinkle the segments with the prepared peel and pour the syrup over the top.
10. Chill for several hours before serving.

Decorate summer desserts with frosted flowers and leaves. Primroses, violets and rose petals; mint, borage and small strawberry leaves are all suitable. Choose perfectly shaped specimens, rinse them gently and dry on paper towels. Using a fine paintbrush, cover both sides of the leaves or petals with lightly beaten egg white, then dip them in caster sugar. Place on non-stick silicone paper and leave to dry for 1-2 hours.

CLOCKWISE FROM THE LEFT: Exotic fruit medley; Gooseberry cream; Orange and grapefruit special.

Summer Pudding

Serves 6
750 g (1¾ lb) mixed fruit (loganberries, blackcurrants, redcurrants, blackberries, strawberries, raspberries)
150 ml (¼ pint) water
100 g (4 oz) caster sugar
8 slices slightly stale white bread, crusts removed

Preparation time: *30 minutes, plus chilling overnight*
Cooking time: *10 minutes*

This is a classic English pudding which was served as far back as the 18th century to people who were not allowed rich desserts. It is a beautifully flavoured dish which uses the best of the English summer fruits. You can also make a spring pudding by adding some tender stewed rhubarb with the early soft fruits, or add a higher proportion of stewed blackberries and some eating apples to make an autumn pudding.

1. Place the fruit and water in a heavy pan with the sugar. Cook gently for 10 minutes. If using strawberries or raspberries add them after the rest of the fruit has been cooked to prevent them disintegrating.
2. Strain the fruit, reserving the cooking juice until later.
3. Cut a circle from one of the slices of bread to line the base of a 900 ml (1½ pint) pudding basin. Cut sufficient wedges of bread to line the sides of the basin. Use scraps of bread to fill any gaps in the bread lining.
4. Dip each piece of this bread into the reserved juice and line the basin. Fill with half the fruit, place another layer of bread on top, then pour in the rest of the fruit and top with another layer of bread.
5. Spoon over any remaining fruit juice.
6. Put a plate that just fits inside the basin's rim on the pudding and put several heavy weights on top. Chill overnight. F
7. Turn the pudding on to a serving dish and serve with a jug of cream.
F Cover and freeze for up to 6 months. Thaw overnight in the refrigerator.

Poires Pralinées

225 g (8 oz) sugar
600 ml (1 pint) water
few strips of lemon rind
4 ripe, even-sized dessert pears
300 ml (½ pint) double cream
100 g (4 oz) Praline (page 72) finely ground

Preparation time: 10 minutes, plus cooling
Cooking time: 15 minutes

Choose large round pears like Comice or Williams for this dish rather than the slimmer Conference pears. It is much easier to make them stand up.

1. Put the sugar and the water in a heavy-based pan over a gentle heat and stir with a wooden spoon until the sugar dissolves. Add the lemon rind.
2. Bring the syrup to the boil, then reduce the heat and simmer for 2 minutes.
3. Peel the pears but leave their stalks on. Core the pears from underneath so that the hole does not show. Poach the pears for 10 minutes, turning occasionally so they cook evenly. Leave them in the syrup until cold. F
4. Lift the pears out of the syrup with a slotted spoon and leave to drain completely. Place either in 1 large or 4 individual serving dishes.
5. Whip the double cream until it is stiff and fold in half the praline. Cover the pears completely with the cream.
6. Sprinkle the remaining praline over the pears and serve.
F Pour into a rigid container with 1-2½ cm (½-1 inch) headspace for expansion and freeze for up to 6 months. Thaw for 3-4 hours at room temperature.

Green and Gold Salad

Serves 6
100 g (4 oz) sugar
150 ml (¼ pint) water
juice of ½ lemon
2 tablespoons Chartreuse
1 small Ogen melon
2 passion fruit
225 g (8 oz) green seedless grapes, peeled
2 kiwi fruit, peeled and sliced

Preparation time: 40 minutes, plus chilling

To make melon balls it is worth buying a food baller to make perfectly round shapes. A melon baller normally has a handle with a cup on one or both ends and comes in different sizes. To make melon balls, cut the melon in half and scrape out all the seeds. Push the baller, cup shape downwards into the flesh. Rotate the cup in the flesh to make a complete ball. Lift out and transfer to a dish. Pieces of leftover melon flesh can be chopped or puréed and used for another dish.

1. Dissolve the sugar in the water in a heavy saucepan over a medium heat, stirring all the time. Bring to the boil and boil for 2-3 minutes. Remove from the heat.
2. Let the syrup cool, add the lemon juice and Chartreuse and pour into a serving bowl.
3. Cut the melon in half, discard the pips, and scoop out melon balls.
4. Cut the passion fruit in half and spoon out the flesh.
5. Mix the grapes, melon balls, slices of kiwi fruit and the passion fruit together carefully in the syrup and chill in the refrigerator. A
A Can be prepared the previous day, covered tightly with clingfilm and kept chilled.

Rhubarb with Ginger

Serves 6
225 g (8 oz) sugar
300 ml (½ pint) water
1 kg (2 lb) rhubarb, washed
75 g (3 oz) stem ginger, finely chopped

Preparation time: 10 minutes, plus cooling
Cooking time: 15-20 minutes

1. Dissolve the sugar and water in a pan over a gentle heat. Bring to the boil.
2. Top and tail the rhubarb. Remove the stringy skin. Cut into 5 cm (2 inch) lengths.
3. Add the rhubarb and the ginger to the syrup, reserving 2 or 3 pieces of ginger for decoration. Simmer gently for 15 minutes.
4. Pour the fruit mixture into a serving dish and leave to cool. A F
5. Decorate with pieces of stem ginger. Serve with ice cream or whipped cream.
A Can be prepared the previous day, covered tightly with clingfilm and kept chilled.
F Pour into a rigid container with 1-2½ cm (½-1 inch) space for expansion and freeze for up to 3 months. Thaw for 4-5 hours at room temperature.

CLOCKWISE FROM BOTTOM LEFT: Summer pudding; Poires pralinées; Green and gold salad.

Summer Shortcake Gâteau

Serves 8
150 g (5 oz) butter
75 g (3 oz) caster sugar
grated rind of 1 lemon
1 egg yolk
225 g (8 oz) plain flour
450 ml (¾ pint) double cream, whipped
225 g (8 oz) soft fruits, in season
icing sugar, for dusting

Preparation time: 30 minutes, plus cooling
Cooking time: 15-20 minutes
Oven: 180°C, 350°F, Gas Mark 4

1. Cream the butter and sugar together in a mixing bowl until soft and fluffy. Stir in the grated lemon rind and the egg yolk. Fold in the flour and knead to a soft dough.
2. Divide the dough into 3. Roll out on a lightly floured board then roll out each piece between 2 pieces of non-stick silicone paper to make a circle 20 cm (8 inches) in diameter. Remove the top piece of paper from each circle, crimp the edges with floured fingertips and prick the circles all over with a fork.
3. Set each circle on a lightly greased baking sheet and bake in a preheated oven until lightly golden.
4. Leave to cool for 2-5 minutes. Divide one circle of shortcake into 8 equal sections.
5. Lift all the shortcake layers off the paper and leave them on a wire tray until completely cool.
6. Sandwich the two uncut layers with one third of the cream and some soft fruit, reserving some for the top.
7. Put the remaining cream into a piping bag fitted with a rose nozzle. Pipe small rosettes of cream over the top of the gâteau, then pipe 8 equally spaced large rosettes of cream on top of them. Prop a shortcake section against each one. Pipe 1 large rosette of cream in the middle of the gâteau. Decorate with soft fruit; dust with icing sugar. Serve within 1-2 hours once assembled.

Flambéed Pineapple

90 g (3½ oz) caster sugar
grated rind and juice of 1 orange
juice of ½ lemon
40 g (1½ oz) unsalted butter
4 thick slices fresh pineapple
2 tablespoons Kirsch (or rum)

Preparation time: 2 minutes
Cooking time: 15 minutes

1. Put the sugar, grated rind and juices in a frying pan. Bring to the boil slowly, stirring until the sugar dissolves and the mixture thickens to a syrup.
2. Lower the heat and add the butter. Swirl it around the pan until melted.
3. Add the pineapple slices and cook them gently for about 10 minutes until heated through, turning them once, and basting them regularly with the syrup. Remove the pan from the heat and lift each slice out of the pan separately with a slotted spoon and place on warmed individual serving dishes.
4. Pour the Kirsch or rum into the pan. Set alight to the syrup carefully and pour it, still flaming, over the pineapple slices. Serve immediately.

Tropical Brûlée

Serves 6
1 egg
2 egg yolks
40 g (1½ oz) vanilla flavoured caster sugar
1½ teaspoons plain flour
450 ml (¾ pint) double cream
1 small mango, peeled, stoned and sliced
1 small orange, peeled, segmented and pith and skin removed
1 small banana, peeled and sliced on the slant and tossed in lemon juice
250 g (9 oz) granulated sugar
120 ml (4 fl oz) water
slices of angelica, to decorate

Preparation time: 20 minutes, plus chilling
Cooking time: about 5 minutes

1. Put a shallow 20 cm (8 inch) dish in the freezer and leave for 30 minutes.
2. Beat the egg, egg yolks, caster sugar and flour together in a mixing bowl.
3. Place the cream in a saucepan and bring it just to boiling point. Pour it into the mixture in a thin stream, stirring constantly to combine the ingredients.
4. Pour the custard into the top of a double boiler. Heat gently, stirring constantly until the custard thickens.
5. Pour the custard into the cold dish. Leave to cool.
6. Arrange the slices of fruit decoratively on top of the cold custard.
7. Place the granulated sugar and the water in a heavy-based pan and, using a wooden spoon, stir over a gentle heat until the sugar dissolves. Bring to the boil and boil until the syrup becomes a golden caramel. Spoon quickly over the fruit, working fast otherwise the caramel will set. Allow to cool. Decorate with angelica.

FROM THE TOP: Summer shortcake gâteau; Tropical brûlée.

Light Fantastic

Meringue Chantilly

Serves 6
few drops of vanilla essence
150 ml (¼ pint) double cream
vanilla sugar, to taste
25 g (1 oz) flaked almonds, toasted, to decorate
Swiss meringue:
2 egg whites
120 g (4½ oz) caster sugar

Preparation time: 40 minutes
Cooking time: 1 hour
Oven: 140°C, 275°F, Gas Mark 1

1. Line 2 baking sheets with lightly greased and floured greaseproof paper, or use non-stick silicone paper.
2. Prepare the Swiss meringue. Place the egg whites in a bowl and whisk them until they are stiff.
3. Gradually whisk in half the sugar until the mixture is thick and glossy.
4. Carefully fold in the remaining sugar.
5. Carefully fold the vanilla essence into the Swiss meringue mixture.
6. Spoon the meringue into a large piping bag fitted with a large star nozzle, and pipe 12 even-size swirls on to the prepared baking sheets.
7. Bake in a preheated oven for about 1 hour or until crisp and lightly coloured.
8. Cool on a wire tray and peel off the paper. Ⓐ Ⓕ
9. To make the filling, whip the cream until thick, add vanilla sugar to taste and sandwich pairs of meringues together. Decorate with the toasted almonds.
Ⓐ The meringues can be made 4 days in advance and stored in an airtight tin.
Ⓕ Pack in rigid containers and freeze for up to 3 months. Thaw at room temperature for 1 hour.

Ginger Delight

Serves 6
100 g (4 oz) trifle sponge cakes, cut into cubes
120 ml (4 fl oz) ginger wine
65 g (2½ oz) strawberry jam
300 ml (½ pint) milk
450 ml (¾ pint) double cream
4 egg yolks, beaten
75 g (3 oz) caster sugar
1 tablespoon cornflour
1 pinch cinnamon
To decorate:
12 ratafias
1 piece crystallized stem ginger, finely sliced

Preparation time: 25 minutes, plus cooling
Cooking time: 15 minutes

For extra ginger flavour, sprinkle finely chopped stem ginger over the sponge.

1. Arrange the sponge cakes in the base of a trifle dish. Moisten with ginger wine. Spread the strawberry jam on top.
2. In a small heavy pan, scald the milk and 150 ml (¼ pint) of the double cream. Mix the egg yolks with 50 g (2 oz) of the sugar and the cornflour in a mixing bowl. Add the hot milk and cream to the sweetened egg yolks, stirring all the time. Return the mixture to a clean pan. Heat gently until thickened, stirring constantly. Pour the hot custard over the jam. Leave on one side to cool, then chill in the refrigerator.
3. Whip the remaining cream with the cinnamon and remaining sugar. Pipe the cream on top of the custard.
4. Decorate with ratafias and ginger.

FROM THE LEFT: Meringue chantilly; Ginger delight.

Oeufs à la Neige

300 ml (½ pint) milk
40 g (1½ oz) vanilla sugar
Meringue islands:
4 egg whites
225 g (8 oz) caster sugar
Custard:
4 egg yolks
2 oz caster sugar

Preparation time: 15-20 minutes, plus chilling
Cooking time: 20-30 minutes

1. Simmer the milk and sugar together.
2. Whisk the egg whites until they stand in firm peaks. Add half the sugar, 1 tablespoon at a time, whisking between each addition until stiff and glossy. Fold in the remaining sugar.
3. Scoop tablespoons of the meringue mixture and slide them on to the milk and simmer. Cook for about 3 minutes, turning them over once.
4. Using a slotted draining spoon, lift the meringue islands out and drain them on a paper towel. Continue poaching a few at a time until all the meringue mixture has been cooked.
5. Strain the milk and prepare the custard. Whisk the egg yolks with the caster sugar until the mixture is thick. Pour the strained milk into the egg mixture, stirring constantly.
6. Return the mixture to the pan and stir continuously over a low heat, without boiling, until it thickens and coats the back of the spoon. Cool and pour into a serving dish. Place the poached meringues on the surface of the custard in a mound.

Crème Caramel

250 ml (8 fl oz) full cream milk
1 egg
2 egg yolks
100 g (4 oz) vanilla sugar
100 g (4 oz) caster sugar
pinch of cream of tartar

Preparation time: 20 minutes, plus cooling
Cooking time: 40 minutes
Oven: 160°C, 325°F, Gas Mark 3

Vanilla pods are used to flavour ice creams, custards and milk puddings. Store them in a jar of caster sugar to make vanilla sugar and leave for 1-2 weeks. The pods can be rinsed, dried and reused several times. Top up the jar with more caster sugar when required and shake to combine with the flavoured sugar.

1. Heat the milk in a saucepan over a gentle heat until it reaches simmering point. Whisk the egg, egg yolks and vanilla sugar together in a mixing bowl then beat in the hot milk. Leave to cool.
2. Place the sugar, cream of tartar and a little water in a separate pan and boil to a mid-amber caramel 160°C/320°F on a sugar thermometer (page 9). Pour into 4 dariole moulds, or one 600 ml (1 pint) mould.
3. Strain the custard, then pour it into the moulds, and stand them in a large roasting tin in 1 cm (½ inch) cold water. Cover with a double layer of foil to prevent a skin forming. Bake in a preheated oven for 40 minutes. Remove from the oven and cool in the tin.
4. When the custards have cooled a little, turn them into individual dishes or 1 large serving dish.

1. Brush four 150 ml (¼ pint) soufflé dishes with the melted butter. Dust with 1 tablespoon of the caster sugar and place in the freezer.
2. Heat the rind, tangerine juice and 65 g (2½ oz) of the caster sugar to simmering point. Blend the arrowroot and water together and whisk into the hot juice, stirring until it thickens. Cool slightly, then beat in the egg yolks.
3. Whisk the egg whites with the remaining 1 tablespoon of caster sugar until stiff and fold the whites into the tangerine mixture.
4. Pour into the prepared soufflé dishes and smooth the tops with a palette knife.
5. Bake in a preheated oven for 10 minutes. Serve immediately.

Madeira Syllabub

300 ml (½ pint) double cream
65 g (2½ oz) caster sugar
1 lemon
50 ml (2 fl oz) Madeira
To decorate:
julienne of lemon rind
lemon balm

Preparation time: 10 minutes

Sweet sherry can be used instead of Madeira.

1. Whip the double cream and sugar until it holds its shape on the whisk.
2. Grate the rind of half the lemon then squeeze the juice from the whole fruit. Combine with the Madeira.
3. Whisk the rind, juice and Madeira into the cream, a little at a time, until the syllabub holds its shape on the whisk. Ⓐ Spoon into 4 wine glasses. Decorate with the julienne and the lemon balm and serve accompanied by Sand Biscuits (page 59).
Ⓐ Can be prepared to this stage up to 3 hours in advance and stored in the refrigerator.

Citrus Soufflé

10 g (¼ oz) unsalted butter, melted
65 g (2½ oz) caster sugar, plus 2 tablespoons
grated rind of 2 tangerines
150 ml (5 fl oz) tangerine juice (about 4 tangerines)
20 g (¾ oz) arrowroot
2 tablespoons cold water
2 eggs, separated

Preparation time: 20 minutes
Cooking time: 15 minutes
Oven: 230°C, 450°F, Gas Mark 8

Other soft citrus fruit (the easy peelers) like mandarins and satsumas can be used instead of tangerines in this recipe. Tangerines (originally from North Africa) have a lot of pips, mandarins (originally from China) fewer, while satsumas (also oriental) don't have any pips at all.

FROM THE LEFT: Madeira syllabub; Crème caramel.

Nut Meringue Gâteaux

Makes 8 individual gâteaux
100 g (4 oz) sugar
85 ml (3 fl oz) water
2 egg whites
100 g (4 oz) butter, softened
3 quantities Praline (right)
Nut meringue:
4 egg whites
250 g (9 oz) caster sugar
few drops of vanilla essence
½ teaspoon lemon juice
100 g (4 oz) almonds, blanched, toasted and ground

Preparation time: 1¼ hours
Cooking time: 30 minutes
Oven: 180°C, 350°F, Gas Mark 4

1. Line 2 baking sheets with non-stick silicone or lightly greased greaseproof paper and draw sixteen 7.5 cm (3 inch) circles.
2. Make the nut meringue. Whisk the egg whites until stiff, then add the sugar 1 tablespoon at a time, whisking continuously until the mixture is thick and holds its shape on the whisk. Fold in the vanilla essence, lemon juice and nuts.
3. Spoon the nut meringue into a piping bag fitted with a plain 5 mm (¼ inch) nozzle.
5. Pipe concentric circles to form a disc of meringue following the drawn line as a guide. Bake in a preheated oven for about 1 hour or until crisp and lightly coloured. Allow to cool on a wire rack.
6. Place the sugar and water in a heavy-based pan and dissolve over a low heat without boiling. Once dissolved, bring to the boil without stirring, and boil until it reaches hard ball stage, 121°C/250°F, on a sugar thermometer (page 9).
7. Meanwhile, whisk the egg whites until stiff. When the syrup is ready, pour it in a steady slow stream on to the egg whites, beating continuously until mixture is cool.
8. Cream the butter until soft and gradually beat in the cooled mixture.
9. Once the nut meringue discs are completely cool Ⓐ Ⓕ sandwich pairs together with the butter cream and spread more over the sides, reserving some for decoration.
10. Roll the sides of each gâteau into the praline, gently pressing it on to the surface.
11. Spoon the remaining butter cream into a piping bag fitted with a small star nozzle. Pipe small stars or rosettes on the top of each one.
Ⓐ The meringue discs can be made 2-4 days ahead and stored in an airtight container.
Ⓕ Or pack in a rigid container and freeze for up to 3 months. Thaw at room temperature for 1 hour.

Praline

Makes 100 g (4 oz)
50 g (2 oz) sugar
50 g (2 oz) whole almonds

Preparation time: 5 minutes, plus cooling
Cooking time: 10 minutes

1. Put the sugar in a heavy-based pan, add 2 tablespoons water and boil for 3 minutes. Spoon a little of the sugar into a cup of cold water. It should form a soft ball, when pressed together with the fingers.
2. Add the almonds and remove from the heat. Stir with a wooden spoon until the sugar forms a crust round each nut.
3. Return to the heat. Stirring constantly, cook until the sugar has melted and caramelized. Pour on to an oiled plate or work surface and cool for 30 minutes.
4. Break the praline into pieces and grind to a powder. Ⓐ
Ⓐ Praline can be made a week in advance and kept in an airtight container.

Chocolate Mousse

225 g (8 oz) plain chocolate
25 g (1 oz) unsalted butter
3 eggs, separated
2 tablespoons whisky
1 egg white

Preparation time: 25 minutes, plus setting

1. Break the chocolate into small pieces and place in a heatproof bowl with the butter. Stand the bowl over a pan of simmering water until melted.
2. Put 2 tablespoons of melted chocolate on to a piece of greaseproof paper and spread thinly with a palette knife. Leave to set. Beat the egg yolks and whisky into the bowl of chocolate and chill until cool, but do not allow the mixture to set.
3. Whisk all 4 egg whites in a bowl until stiff and fold into the chocolate mixture.
4. Pour into four 150 ml (¼ pint) ramekin dishes or six 100 ml (4 fl oz) chocolate pots. Ⓐ Ⓕ Chill for at least 6 hours until set. Cut the melted chocolate into triangles and decorate the mousses.
Ⓐ Can be prepared the day before and stored in the refrigerator.
Ⓕ Cover and freeze for up to 6 months. Thaw in the refrigerator for 4-5 hours.

FROM THE TOP: Chocolate mousse; Nut meringue gâteaux.

Strawberry Charlotte

Serves 6-8
400 ml (14 fl oz) milk
6 egg yolks
175 (6 oz) caster sugar
2 packets powdered gelatine
75 ml (3 fl oz) hot water
600 g (21 oz) strawberries
250 ml (8 fl oz) double cream
32 sponge fingers
whipped cream, to decorate

Preparation time: *50 minutes, plus setting*
Cooking time: *10 minutes*

1. Heat the milk in a saucepan over a gentle heat to simmering point. Whisk the yolks and sugar in a bowl until light, then pour over the milk and mix well.

2. Return the custard to the rinsed pan and heat without boiling until it coats the back of a wooden spoon. Remove from the heat and pour into a large bowl.

3. Sprinkle the gelatine over the water in a small heat-proof bowl. Stand the bowl in a pan of hot water and heat gently, without boiling, and stir until the gelatine has dissolved. Stir the gelatine into the custard.

4. Reserve 6 strawberries for decoration and blend the rest to a purée. Add the purée to the custard. Chill until on the point of setting.

5. Whip the cream until it holds its shape and fold in the custard.

6. Line a charlotte mould with foil. Arrange the sponge fingers, sugared side outwards, on the bottom and round the sides of the tin, cutting to fit where necessary, and fill with the charlotte mixture. Ⓐ Ⓕ Chill for 4 hours or overnight.

7. To serve, unmould the charlotte then carefully remove the foil. Decorate with whipped cream and the reserved strawberries.

Ⓐ Wrap in clingfilm and store for 24 hours in the refrigerator.

Ⓕ Overwrap and freeze for 3 months. Thaw overnight in the refrigerator.

FROM THE LEFT: Strawberry charlotte; Caribbean soufflé.

Soufflé Rothschild

50 g (2 oz) crystallized fruit
25 ml (1 fl oz) Orange Curaçao
25 g (1 oz) unsalted butter
50 g (2 oz) caster sugar, plus 1 teaspoon
4 eggs, separated
25 g (1 oz) cornflour
150 ml (5 fl oz) milk

Preparation time: 20 minutes
Cooking time: 30 minutes
Oven: 190°C, 375°F, Gas Mark 5

1. Finely chop the crystallized fruit and mix with the Orange Curaçao. Leave to macerate.
2. Melt 10 g (¼ oz) of the butter and use to brush the inside of a 1.5 litre (2½ pint) soufflé dish. Coat with 1 teaspoon of the caster sugar.
3. Blend the cornflour with 2 tablespoons of the milk.
4. Heat the rest of the milk to boiling point with the sugar, pour on to the cornflour and mix together well.
5. Pour the cornflour mixture into the rinsed pan and heat gently, stirring all the time, until the mixture becomes thick. Remove from the heat. Beat the mixture so that it forms a smooth, thick sauce.
6. Beat the egg yolks and the remaining butter, cut into small pieces, into the sauce until smooth. Transfer the mixture to a large bowl.

7. Fold in the Orange Curaçao and the crystallized fruits.
8. Whisk the egg whites until stiff. Stir 1 tablespoon of beaten egg white into the custard. Fold in the remaining egg white.
9. Pour the mixture into the prepared soufflé dish. Smooth the top with a palette knife. Bake in a pre-heated oven for 30 minutes. Dust with icing sugar and serve at once.

Caribbean Soufflé

25 g (1 oz) unsalted butter
60 g (2¼ oz) caster sugar, plus 1 tablespoon
4 eggs, separated
20 g (¾ oz) flour
150 ml (¼ pint) milk
2 bananas, peeled
50 ml (2 fl oz) rum
Sauce:
3 egg yolks
50 g (2 oz) caster sugar
40 ml (1½ fl oz) rum
1 tablespoon orange juice
icing sugar, to dredge

Preparation time: 30 minutes
Cooking time: 40 minutes
Oven: 190°C, 375°F, Gas Mark 5

1. Melt 10 g (¼ oz) of the butter and use to brush the inside of a 1.25 litre (2¼ pint) soufflé dish. Dust with 1 tablespoon of the caster sugar and chill.
2. Whisk the egg yolks, 40 g (1½ oz) of the caster sugar and the flour in a mixing bowl. Heat the milk and pour over the mixture. Blend thoroughly. Pour into a clean pan and heat gently without boiling, stirring constantly, until the custard thickens. Beat in the remaining butter.
3. Slice 1 banana and leave to marinate in the rum. Blend the second banana to a purée and add to the custard.
4. Whisk the egg whites and remaining caster sugar until stiff. Fold the rum and banana slices into the custard, then fold in the egg whites.
5. Pour into the prepared soufflé dish. Smooth the top with a palette knife, then bake in a preheated oven for 30 minutes.
6. Meanwhile, make the sauce. Whisk the yolks and sugar until creamy. Add the rum and orange juice. Stand the bowl containing the yolks and sugar mixture over a pan of simmering water. Whisk until the sauce becomes light and fluffy.
7. Dredge with icing sugar then serve the soufflé immediately, accompanied by the sauce.

Bavarian Coffee Cream

200 ml (7 fl oz) milk
3 egg yolks
75 g (3 oz) sugar
15 g (½ oz) powdered gelatine
50 ml (2 fl oz) hot water
120 ml (4 fl oz) strong black coffee
120 ml (4 fl oz) double cream, whipped
To decorate:
whipped cream
nasturtium flowers

Preparation time: *20 minutes, plus chilling overnight*
Cooking time: *10 minutes*

1. Heat the milk in a saucepan over a gentle heat to simmering point. Whisk the yolks and sugar in a mixing bowl until light then pour the milk into the yolks. Mix together well.
2. Return the custard to the rinsed pan and heat without boiling until it coats the back of a wooden spoon. Remove the pan from the heat and pour the custard into a deep baking tin.
3. Sprinkle the gelatine over the hot water in a small heatproof bowl. Stand the bowl in a pan of hot water and heat gently, without boiling, and stir until the gelatine has dissolved. Remove the bowl from the heat and stir the gelatine into the custard. Add the black coffee, then chill until on the point of setting.
4. Fold the cream into the custard. Pour the bavarois into a 900 ml (1½ pint) mould. Cover and refrigerate, overnight if possible. Ⓐ Ⓕ
5. Dip the mould in hot water for a few seconds then turn on to a serving dish and decorate.
Ⓐ Can be kept for 2 days in the refrigerator.
Ⓕ Make the bavarois in a freezer container, wrap closely and freeze for up to 6 months. Thaw overnight in the refrigerator.

FROM THE LEFT: Bavarian coffee cream; Raspberry trifles.

Mini Sponge Creams

120 g (4½ oz) sponge cake
40 g (1½ oz) tawny marmalade
40 g (1½ oz) raspberry jam
16 ratafias
150 ml (¼ pint) Amontillado sherry
300 ml (½ pint) double cream
65 g (2½ oz) caster sugar
3 tablespoons Madeira
3 tablespoons brandy
rind and juice of ½ lemon
20 g (¾ oz) redcurrant jelly, to decorate
angelica, to decorate

Preparation time: *30 minutes*

Raspberry Trifles

65 g (2½ oz) sugar
50 ml (2 fl oz) water
25 ml (1 fl oz) raspberry liqueur or Kirsch
20 sponge fingers
4 ratafias
4 heaped teaspoons raspberry jam
fresh raspberries, to decorate
Crème Anglaise:
3 egg yolks
60 g (2¼ oz) vanilla sugar
250 ml (8 fl oz) full cream milk
Crème Chantilly:
150 ml (5 fl oz) double cream
25 ml (1 fl oz) egg white
25 g (1 oz) caster or vanilla sugar

Preparation time: 30 minutes, plus standing and chilling
Cooking time: 5 minutes

1. Boil the sugar and water in a heavy-based saucepan until the sugar dissolves. Cool, then add the raspberry liqueur or Kirsch.
2. Break the sponge fingers into several pieces and arrange in a bowl with the ratafias. Pour over the syrup.
3. Spoon half the sponge fingers into the bottoms of 4 glass dishes. Spoon the raspberry jam over the top and cover with the remaining biscuits and ratafias.
4. Meanwhile make the crème Anglaise. In a bowl, whisk the yolks and sugar until creamy. Gently heat the milk in a saucepan to simmering point, then pour the hot milk over the egg yolk mixture.
5. Pour into the rinsed pan. Heat gently, stirring continuously, until the sauce coats the back of a wooden spoon. Take care as it will curdle if it is boiled. **A**
6. Pour the hot crème Anglaise into the 4 glass dishes. Stand for 15 minutes to cool, then chill for 15 minutes.
7. Prepare the crème Chantilly. Put the cream in a mixing bowl, add the egg white and whisk until the cream begins to hold its shape on the whisk.
8. Add the sugar. Whisk until the cream is smooth and holds its shape.
9. Fit a piping bag with a large star nozzle and fill with the crème Chantilly. Decorate the top edge of the 4 trifles with rosettes of cream and top each one with a raspberry. Chill for a few minutes before serving.
A Crème Anglaise can be prepared 2-3 days in advance. Pour into a clean bowl, cover and keep in the refrigerator.

1. Divide the sponge into 8 pieces. Spread marmalade on 4 of them and raspberry jam on the remainder.
2. Arrange a piece of jam-coated sponge and a piece of marmalade-coated sponge in each of 4 glass coupes. Place 4 ratafias on each one. Carefully spoon the Amontillado sherry on top.
3. Whisk the double cream with sugar until it holds its shape on the whisk.
4. Combine the Madeira, brandy, lemon rind and juice. Whisk into the cream until the cream is stiff.
5. Spoon the cream over the 4 coupes. It should just reach the top of the bowls. Smooth the surface with the back of a knife.
6. Stir the redcurrant jelly into a teaspoon of hot water until dissolved. Using a piping bag and a writing nozzle, pipe a design with the melted jelly on the top of each sponge cream. Decorate with pieces of angelica.

Meringue and Apricot Layer Cake

Serves 6
100 g (4 oz) dried apricots, soaked overnight
25 g (1 oz) caster sugar
300 ml (½ pint) double cream, whipped
Nut meringue:
4 egg whites
250 g (9 oz) caster sugar
few drops of vanilla essence
½ teaspoon lemon juice
100 g (4 oz) almonds, blanched, toasted and ground
1 × 300 g (11 oz) can apricot halves, to decorate

Preparation time: 40 minutes, plus soaking overnight
Cooking time: 40-45 minutes
Oven: 180°C, 350°F, Gas Mark 4

1. Draw two 20 cm (8 inch) circles on non-stick silicone or lightly greased greaseproof paper and place on 2 baking sheets.
2. Make the nut meringue. Whisk the egg whites until stiff, then add the sugar 1 tablespoon at a time, whisking continuously until the mixture is thick and holds its shape on the whisk.
3. Gently fold in the vanilla essence, lemon juice and ground almonds.
4. Spoon or pipe the nut meringue on to the prepared baking sheets, following the marked circles.
5. Bake in a preheated oven for 40-45 minutes until crisp and lightly coloured. Leave to cool on a wire tray for 15 minutes, then remove the paper. Ⓐ Ⓕ
6. To make the filling, simmer the soaked apricots in their liquid until they are tender and have reduced to a thick purée. Cool and sweeten to taste.
7. Reserve half the cream and mix the remainder with the apricot purée.
8. Sandwich the meringues with the apricot cream and decorate the top with piped cream rosettes and and apricots.
Ⓐ The meringue rounds can be made 4 days in advance and stored in an airtight tin.
Ⓕ Pack in rigid containers and freeze for up to 3 months. Thaw at room temperature for 1 hour.

Nutty Mousse

100 g (4 oz) hazelnuts
4 eggs, separated
100 g (4 oz) caster sugar, plus 1 tablespoon
1 teaspoon cornflour
300 ml (½ pint) milk
15 g (½ oz) powdered gelatine
50 ml (2 fl oz) water
To decorate:
double cream, whipped

Preparation time: 35 minutes, plus setting
Cooking time: 15 minutes
Oven: 200°C, 400°F, Gas Mark 6

1. Spread the hazelnuts on a baking sheet and roast in the oven for 15 minutes. Remove from the oven, cool slightly, then rub off the skins. Reserve 8 for decoration and grind the rest to a powder.
2. Place the egg yolks, 50 g (2 oz) of the caster sugar and the flour in a bowl and whisk until creamy.
3. Heat the milk then pour over the yolk and sugar mixture. Blend thoroughly. Pour into a clean pan and heat gently, stirring constantly, until the custard coats the back of a wooden spoon.
4. Sprinkle the gelatine over the water in a small heat-proof bowl. Stand the bowl in a pan of hot water and stir until the gelatine has dissolved. Remove from the heat. Whisk into the custard, then pour the custard into a bowl. Add the ground nuts and cool until the custard is on the point of setting.
5. Cut out a sheet of non-stick silicone paper or foil 55×15 cm (22×6 inches). Fasten it around a 15 cm (6 inch) soufflé dish to form a collar 7.5 cm (3 inches) above the rim of the dish. Secure the paper.
6. Whisk the egg whites and remaining caster sugar until very stiff. Fold into the hazelnut flavoured custard and pour into the mould. Ⓐ Ⓕ Chill until set.
7. Remove the paper collar and pipe on cream rosettes and decorate with the reserved nuts.
Ⓐ Can be made 24 hours in advance.
Ⓕ Open-freeze, then leaving the collar on, wrap in a polythene bag and freeze for up to 2 months. Make a foil collar if you are going to freeze the mousse. Thaw overnight in the refrigerator.

FROM THE TOP: Nutty mousse; Meringue and apricot layer cake.

Index